Job Loss from Imports: Measuring the Costs

Job Loss from Imports: Measuring the Costs

Lori G. Kletzer

Institute for International Economics
Washington, DC
September 2001

Lori G. Kletzer, visiting fellow, is Associate Professor of Economics at the University of California, Santa Cruz. She formerly worked at the Brookings Institution, the University of Washington, and Williams College and has received research grants from the Andrew W. Mellon Foundation, the National Science Foundation, and the US Department of Labor. She is the author of numerous articles and a forthcoming research monograph on trade, job loss, and employment for the W. E. Upjohn Institute for Employment Research.

INSTITUTE FOR INTERNATIONAL ECONOMICS
1750 Massachusetts Avenue, NW
Washington, DC 20036-1903
(202) 328-9000 FAX: (202) 328-5432
http://www.iie.com

C. Fred Bergsten, *Director*
Brigitte Coulton, *Director of Publications and Web Development*
Brett Kitchen, *Director of Marketing*

Typesetting and printing by Automated Graphic Systems, Inc.
Cover photo: Stephen Simpson/ FPG International

Printed in the United States of America
03 02 01   5 4 3 2 1

Library of Congress Cataloging-in-Publication Data

Kletzer, Lori G.
    Job loss from imports: Measuring the Costs. / Lori G. Kletzer.
        p. cm.
    Includes bibliographical references and index.
    ISBN 0-88132-296-2
    1. Foreign trade and employment.
    2. Labor market. 3. International trade.
    4. Unemployment. I. Title.

HD5710.7 .K54 2001
331.13′7—dc21   2001039388

Contents

Figures

Preface

This book is the second in the Institute's Globalization Balance Sheet (GBS) series, a multiyear family of analyses undertaken to evaluate the impact of international economic integration on the United States. The first study in the series was *Globalization and the Perceptions of American Workers*, by Kenneth F. Scheve and Matthew J. Slaughter, released in early 2001. That analysis documented the fundamental split in American public opinion over globalization and the critical role played by the levels of educational attainment in explaining the sharp cleavage in attitude.

The full GBS series will include a wide-ranging set of studies that measure the underappreciated and underquantified gains and losses from globalization to different groups within the United States, as well as its overall net impact on the country. We will be better able to assess the claims of both proponents and opponents of globalization. More directly, we will be much better situated to address the real losses that can result from the process of increasing global integration. The GBS series is being managed by Senior Fellow J. David Richardson, who has played a major role in the preparation of this volume as he has in all of the other components of the project.

In the heat of the globalization backlash, the domestic labor market consequences of trade-related job loss are a central issue for near-term US international economic (especially trade) policy. Trade liberalization has long been a focal point for anxiety about job insecurity. While considerable economic evidence shows much of that focus to be misplaced, in the sense that trade ranks well behind technological change and immigration as a source of job loss and declining real wages for less-skilled workers, anxiety over trade and jobs remains a real and potent political force. This book documents that Americans are wise to be anxious about losing jobs and wages, for trade as well as other reasons. Through an analysis of a nationally representative sample of displaced workers, author Lori G. Kletzer shows that there is an identifiable group of workers for whom import-competing job loss is very costly. Workers vulnerable to import-competing job loss experience considerable difficulty regaining employment and they experience large and persistent earnings losses upon reemployment. But so do all displaced manufacturing workers. The central message of this book is that it is not import competition per se that determines the difficulty of adjustment. For most displaced workers, what matters is the kind of job lost and the kind of job regained. *Why* the job was lost does not matter much at all. If workers and consequences are alike, across differing causes of job loss such as increasing foreign competition, technological change, downsizing and restructuring, then policymakers should consider adjustment policy for all displaced workers and broaden program eligibility beyond "trade-displaced workers."

Kletzer bases her conclusions on three key findings. First, workers displaced from import-competing manufacturing industries are similar to other displaced manufacturing workers with respect to age, educational attainment, and job tenure. Like other displaced manufacturing workers, they are slightly older, notably less educated and with longer job tenure than workers displaced from nonmanufacturing industries. These characteristics are associated with difficult labor market adjustments. Second, while the transition to a new job is difficult for these workers, the difficulties do not end with the new job. Two-thirds of the reemployed workers earn less on their new job than they did on their old job, and one-quarter of them indeed experience earnings losses in excess of 30 percent. This distribution of earnings losses is very similar to that found for all displaced manufacturing workers as a group.

Third, the industry where workers are reemployed matters a great deal for understanding the differences in earnings losses. About one-third of all import-competing displaced workers are reemployed back in manufacturing. Another one-third are reemployed in the nonmanufacturing sector. The remaining one-third were not reemployed at all when surveyed. Importantly, for displaced manufacturing workers, regaining employment in manufacturing greatly reduces earnings losses.

Our reading of the globalization backlash is that the political process needs to do a much better job of recognizing the costs to individual workers of freer trade and the scope of their losses. It should put into place credible, effective government mechanisms for easing the necessary labor market adjustments. Future progress on trade liberalization may indeed be conditioned on a more active domestic labor market policy agenda, including new worker adjustment assistance programs—such as the wage insurance idea presented briefly in this book.

The Institute for International Economics is a private nonprofit institution for the study and discussion of international economic policy. Its purpose is to analyze important issues in that area and develop and communicate practical new approaches for dealing with them. The Institute is completely nonpartisan.

The Institute is funded largely by philanthropic foundations. Major institutional grants are now being received from the William M. Keck, Jr. Foundation and the Starr Foundation. A number of other foundations and private corporations contribute to the highly diversified financial resources of the Institute. Partial funding for the Institute's Globalization Balance Sheet series is being provided by the Toyota Motor Corporation, in light of the great interest in these issues in both the United States and Japan. The Andrew W. Mellon Foundation is also supporting these studies. About 31 percent of the Institute's resources in our latest fiscal year were provided by contributors outside the United States, including about 18 percent from Japan.

The Board of Directors bears overall responsibility for the Institute and gives general guidance and approval to its research program—including the identification of topics that are likely to become important over the medium run (one to three years), and which should be addressed by the Institute. The Director, working closely with the staff and outside Advisory Committee, is responsible for the development of particular projects and makes the final decision to publish an individual study.

The Institute hopes that its studies and other activities will contribute to building a stronger foundation for international economic policy around the world. We invite readers of these publications to let us know how they think we can best accomplish this objective.

C. Fred Bergsten
Director
August 2001

Acknowledgments

This study has been improved by the thoughtful and helpful comments and suggestions of a number of scholars. I am grateful to Susan Collins, Kimberly Elliott, Gordon Hanson, Louis Jacobson, Howard Lewis, Howard Rosen, and Gregory Schoepfle who read a preliminary draft of the manuscript and provided written comments. A special note of thanks to J. David Richardson for his extensive comments on an earlier draft and unflagging support for my research. I also thank Anne Polivka and Rosemary Hyson for their data suggestions and comments, and C. Fred Bergsten, Catherine Mann, Adam Posen, and related researchers on the Globalization Balance Sheet project at the Institute for International Economics for their suggestions. Maria Unterrainer provided excellent research assistance. Brigitte Coulton, Madona Devasahayam, and Marla Banov provided superb editorial assistance in preparing this book for publication.

This book was written while I was a visiting fellow at the Institute for International Economics and I thank all my colleagues there for providing a stimulating environment for thinking about these issues.

1

Introduction: Focusing on Displaced Workers

Increasing economic integration across countries (the international flows of goods, services, people, and capital commonly known as "globalization") produces large gains—particularly for the US economy as a whole. Productivity is enhanced when goods and services are produced in countries with a comparative advantage and then traded. Consumers get lower prices and improved welfare. Global competition helps restrain price inflation and spurs innovation. In turn, innovation spurs globalization. These gains, although widespread and widely touted, are not always well understood.

But globalization also has costs. And these costs tend to be concentrated where the benefits are widespread. Producers in domestic industries whose products compete with imports (hereafter, import-competing industries) face falling profits and see their business threatened by the lower-cost competition. Workers in import-competing industries lose jobs or face downward wage pressure. Other workers fear job loss from heightened global competitive pressure and the perceived ease with which firms can relocate production. Americans are aware of both the pluses and minuses of continued globalization, as seen in public opinion polls (see Program on International Policy Attitudes 2000; Scheve and Slaughter 2001). But for many years, the "free trade" debate in the public policy arena has emphasized the benefits of trade and ignored the costs.

This one-sided emphasis has been stopped—almost dead in its tracks—by the globalization backlash. How can the public policy debate be started and expanded? To move forward again on the path of economic integration, it is time for the policy debate to include a better understanding of the distribution of the costs of globalization. There is broad agreement, at least in principle, on the net benefits of free trade. That says little more than that the (gross) benefits exceed the (gross) costs. Again in principle, the benefits can be used to compensate for the losses, producing a superior societal outcome. One important step in moving toward this outcome, and making these compensations, is to identify who bears the burden of the costs and to measure the size of the burden. This book—part of a larger study of globalization's costs and benefits—seeks to provide this basic information and draw policy conclusions.

Much of the debate about the domestic labor market and free trade has been focused on the number of jobs affected.[1] This focus is unfortunate; these accounting efforts should not form the central focus of the debate on the benefits of free trade or increased economic integration. The economy's level of employment—total number of jobs—is determined more by macroeconomic events and policy than by changes in trade policy or the trade balance.

Important Questions—and Answers

Lost in the misguided debate over the number of jobs created or destroyed by increased economic integration is the really important question: what kind of work will Americans do, as the dynamic US economy continues to change, with more trade and technological advances? Jobs are lost and created, and workers displaced and reemployed, in a dynamic economy. Rather than focus on how many jobs will be affected, we need to understand workers—who they are and *how* they will be affected. Specifically, who are the workers displaced from import-competing industries? What are their characteristics? How do they compare with others who lose their jobs? What happens after displacement? How do they adjust? What can we learn from the pattern of reemployment and earnings that will aid in (re)designing adjustment services?

The research reported here focuses on individual workers, mostly in manufacturing. It builds on a foundation of more than a decade of displacement research. This research has shown that the earnings losses following job dislocation are large and persist over time (see Kletzer 1998b). To examine the costs of import-sensitive job loss, I use results from my earlier industry-level studies of the relationship between increasing foreign competition, employment change, and job loss to develop a defini-

---

1. The North American Free Trade Agreement (NAFTA), starting with its negotiations in the early 1990s and continuing through its current outcomes, has been a prime source for the heated jobs debate. For an early view, see Hufbauer and Schott (1993). For a recent contribution, see Economic Policy Institute (2001).

tion of an import-competing industry and apply that definition to a nationally representative sample of displaced workers. This process yields a sample of import-competing displaced workers. The labeling of "import-competing"—or import-sensitive—job loss thus is according to the industry from which the job was lost. Although I make no strong claims about the precise cause of each worker's job loss, I am confident that the sample captures most of the kinds of jobs Americans feel to be "at risk" from increasing economic integration. My examination of the evidence proceeds through a series of questions, with the answers previewed here:

■ **Question 1:** How can we define import-competing job loss? What can we learn about the scope of job loss from import-sensitive industries? **Answer:** I rank detailed industries (defined at the 3-digit Census of Population Industrial Classification [CIC] level) by their percentage change in import share during the 1979-94 period (from largest positive changes to smallest). Using that ranking, industries in the top 25 percent are defined as the "most" import-competing ones. This industry definition is then applied to the worker-based Displaced Worker Surveys to draw out a sample of import-competing displaced workers, based on an individual's industry of displacement. During the 21-year period from 1979 to 1999, 6.4 million workers were displaced from an import-competing industry; about 17 million were displaced from manufacturing. Import-competing job loss is concentrated in a few large-employment industries: electrical machinery, apparel, motor vehicles, nonelectrical machinery, and blast furnaces.

■ **Question 2:** Do import-competing displaced workers have different characteristics than other manufacturing workers? How do these workers compare with workers displaced from other sectors of the economy? **Answer:** Import-competing workers are similar to other displaced manufacturing workers—slightly older, with virtually no difference in educational attainment or job tenure. The most striking difference between import-competing displaced workers and other displaced manufacturing workers is the degree to which import-competing industries employ and displace women. Women account for 45 percent of import-sensitive displaced workers, relative to 37 percent of the overall manufacturing displaced. Some industries stand out: Women account for 80 percent of those displaced from apparel, 66 percent from footwear, and 76 percent from knitting mills (part of the textiles industry).[2] Thus we see that women dominate the group of displaced workers from these

2. In 1992, women accounted for 77 percent of employment in apparel, 54 percent in footwear, and 67 percent in knitting mills. In 1978, women represented, respectively, 82, 70, and 67 percent of employment in these three industries.

import-competing industries as a result of their strong representation in employment. In comparison with workers displaced from other sectors of the economy (e.g., wholesale and retail trade, utilities, and services), manufacturing workers are slightly older, are notably less educated, have longer job tenure, are somewhat more likely to be a member of a minority group, and are far more likely to be production oriented (blue collar workers).

- **Question 3:** What are the reemployment prospects of import-competing displaced workers? Does the likelihood of reemployment differ by industrial sector?
  Answer: Import-competing displaced workers are a little less likely to be reemployed (63.4 percent were reemployed at their survey date) than other displaced manufacturing workers (65.8 percent were reemployed). Most of this statistically significant difference is accounted for by the lower reemployment rate of women—at 56.2 percent, 13 percentage points lower than the rate for men. Women are heavily employed and displaced from import-competing industries. More generally, manufacturing workers are less likely to be reemployed than nonmanufacturing workers. Some of this difference is accounted for by higher age, less education, longer job tenure, minority status, and gender. There is a remaining gap, with both durable-goods displaced workers less likely to be reemployed (by 4.2 percentage points) and nondurable-goods displaced workers less likely to be reemployed (by 2.7 points) than a worker displaced from a large set of nonmanufacturing industries (including transportation, communications, utilities, wholesale and retail trade, and services), where the reemployment rate was 69 percent.

- **Question 4:** How costly is job displacement, in terms of earnings losses? What do we know about the size and range of these losses? Who are the workers with the largest earnings losses?
  Answer: Among the reemployed, import-competing displaced workers experience sizable average weekly earnings losses of about 13 percent. This large average loss masks considerable variation: 36 percent of import-competing displaced workers report earning the same or more on their new job as they earned on the old job, and 25 percent reported earnings losses of 30 percent or more. This average and distribution are very similar to those for manufacturing workers as a group. Older, less educated, lower-skilled production workers with established tenure on their old job are more likely to suffer earnings losses in excess of 30 percent.

- **Question 5:** Where do workers become reemployed? How accurate is the perception that all reemployment is in the services sector? Do exporting industries account for much reemployment? How important is changing industry in understanding earnings losses?

Answer: The reemployment sector matters a great deal for understanding the variation in earnings losses. Contrary to stereotype, not all displaced manufacturing workers are reemployed at McDonald's. Overall, just 10 percent of reemployed manufacturing workers are in retail trade, and this percentage is similar for import-competing displaced workers. Fifty percent of import-competing workers are reemployed back in manufacturing, and the same percentage holds for manufacturing overall. Export-intensive manufacturing industries do not account for a large share of reemployment. Regaining employment in manufacturing greatly reduces earnings losses. Earnings losses are largest for workers employed in retail trade. Reemployment in the same industry is very important for reducing earnings losses, with half of all these workers reporting very small or no earnings losses.

- **Question 6:** How can the pattern of reemployment inform our policy decisions on the future of worker adjustment programs?

Answer: The pattern of reemployment can reveal how the consequences of job loss vary and how some discernible transitions are better than others. Reemploying some workers in "the right places" might reduce the number of workers who need retraining. The best outcome for many import-competing displaced workers—particularly middle-aged workers with high tenure and a high school education—appears to be a return to their old industry. Their earnings losses will be smaller, for the most part. This outcome suggests tailored job search assistance, to help workers seek reemployment in old industries where skills are transferable. We know that workers can be provided with job-search assistance at a low cost. The patterns found here should also prompt a rethinking of the current focus of assistance on education and retraining (if these policy tools are predicated on reallocating workers to different jobs). Education, skill enhancement, and retraining do help some workers. But for older workers, many of whom are represented in this book, enhancing job skills and retraining will be problematic. Training programs can require higher education levels for entry than many workers have attained, and completing a course can be difficult. Furthermore, the evidence presented here shows that finding a job in a different sector can be very costly; thus, a policy response to economic structural change that depends on reallocating retrained workers across sectors (from the "old" economy to the "new") may not be an answer for all. A more broadly based labor market policy should include active assistance for finding new jobs and short-term financial assistance when the new job pays less than the old.[3]

---

3. A proposed program of "wage insurance" for all displaced workers is discussed in chapter 8 and presented in more detail in Kletzer and Litan (2001).

Informing Future Policymaking

One of the most important findings for policymaking is that, for most displaced workers, what matters is the kind of job lost and the kind of job regained. Why the job was lost does not matter much at all. If workers and consequences are alike, across differing causes of job loss (e.g., increasing foreign competition, technological change, and downsizing), then policymakers should consider adjustment policy for all displaced workers, and broaden program eligibility beyond "trade-displaced workers." A broadly based program is not only justified here by the data, but would also serve to reduce the perception that free trade is a special problem for workers, one that alone needs to be addressed by labor market assistance programs.[4]

Thinking about Trade and the Labor Market

This book complements and extends some of the questions posed in much of the current research on trade and the labor market. During the past 25 years, as the US economy has become more open and integrated, manufacturing employment (particularly of production workers) has declined, real wage growth has been sluggish, and income inequality has increased. These coincident time trends have motivated the creation of an active research literature investigating the link between globalization and major recent US labor market changes. One core question: Is globalization a culprit in the deteriorating economic status of less-skilled workers? In a recent review of the empirical literature, Blanchflower (2000) concludes that globalization is not the major influence in recent labor market changes, but rather one of several important factors. Other key factors are skill-biased technological change, immigration, declining unionization, and declining real minimum wages.[5]

My approach differs from much of the trade and wages literature. First, microevidence on real displaced workers, their characteristics, and post-displacement outcomes is used to measure the domestic impact of trade—in contrast to the most common measures, changes in net industry employment and in industry wages. Second, instead of pursuing ways to disentangle trade from technology, my operating assumption is that all manufacturing industries and their workers are affected similarly by trends in

---

4. One sense in which free trade is different is the political dimension. Trade flows do change as a result of trade liberalization. Job loss resulting from environmental regulation has a similar political dimension. In these cases, where society takes a set of actions that raise overall public welfare, there are important issues of compensation.

5. Interested readers are directed to Kletzer (2001) for a review of the recent literature on international trade and the domestic labor market.

technology, outsourcing, capital deepening, and other related changes. I then infer the effects of extraordinary surges in import competition alone from the differences in outcomes between my samples of import-competing workers and otherwise-displaced manufacturing workers.[6] Such differences turn out to be small, as summarized above.

My questions and approach do not presume increasing economic integration to be the *most* important factor in domestic labor market changes. Nor do I presume that the forces of increasing trade can be separated definitively from other factors. It is very difficult to disentangle technological change from the heightened competitive pressures of globalization (i.e., it is difficult to separate trade from technology). In the main, I attempt to stay out of that fray in this book. My strategy for identifying import-competing industries does not imply that all workers displaced from these industries are displaced by rising imports. The causes of job loss in any industry are broader: technological change, restructuring, shifts in investment, changes in domestic demand. These causes are not my focus. My focus here is on the costs of (any kind of) job loss from import-competing industries.

Before we begin, one note on limitations. This book focuses on job loss associated with trade, and not, for example, multinational investment. The trade focus is mostly on imports, not exports. That emphasis is admittedly one-sided, but it takes on directly the allegation that "imports cost jobs," and I believe this to be one of the most important perceived costs of globalization. As such, this book ignores job gains and the quality of jobs related to trade and investment. Others have written about exports and jobs (see Richardson and Rindal 1995, 1996), and about investment and jobs (see Slaughter and Blonigen 2000).

The book proceeds as follows. I summarize my earlier industry-level research on increasing foreign competition, employment change, and job loss in chapter 2, as a prelude to developing a working definition of an import-competing industry. The trade and job loss data are then described. Applying my definition to the data, I introduce the categorization of manufacturing industries by degree of import sensitivity. The chapter concludes with a discussion of two-way trade.

Chapter 3 examines the characteristics of workers displaced from the most import-sensitive industries, and compares them with other manufacturing workers and workers displaced from industries other than manu-

---

6. Of course, one may quarrel with the assumption. For example, Levinsohn and Petropoulos (2000) show the importance of capital deepening to the textiles industry, whereas for the apparel industry, the key change was outsourcing. But to challenge my results, the critic of this book's way of defining trade-displaced workers needs to prove that technological change, capital deepening, outsourcing, etc., affect import-competing industries in a systematically different way than they have affected the rest of manufacturing or the economy as a whole.

facturing. Chapter 4 turns to the first postdisplacement outcome, reemployment, and reports estimates from a straightforward econometric model of the probability of reemployment. Chapter 5 reports on reemployment earnings and earnings losses, and brings in information from studies that follow the same workers' experience over time. The industrial sectors where workers are reemployed is the topic of chapter 6. Here we see how earnings losses vary by reemployment sector. The importance of regaining employment in the same industry or sector to minimize earnings losses is also examined. Chapter 7 concludes, and discusses in some detail how these findings can inform future policymaking.

2

Defining Import-Competing
Manufacturing Job Loss

This chapter develops a working definition of an import-competing manufacturing industry. That definition will be applied to a nationally representative sample of displaced workers to identify a sample of import-competing displaced workers. Because this is a study of manufacturing jobs and workers, it will be helpful to the narrative to start with an overview of US manufacturing from the late 1970s to the late 1990s. The overview provides some perspective on the definition of import competition.

Manufacturing, in Brief

From the perspective of manufacturing employment, the two decades from the late 1970s to the late 1990s posed one difficulty after another. The sector as a whole was rocked by two recessions, a deep one in the early 1980s and another, not so deep, in the early 1990s; sluggish productivity growth; continued shifts in US consumer demand away from manufactured goods and toward services; technological change, particularly in the form of computer-aided production and design; and an increase in the flows of imports and exports.

Manufacturing employment was in slow but steady decline, from 21 million in 1979 to 18.5 million in 1999. Manufacturing's share of total nonagricultural employment plunged during the same years, from 23.4 to 14.4 percent, while its share of output fell from 22.2 to 16.1 percent. The sector's openness to trade increased dramatically: goods exports as a share of sector gross domestic product (GDP) increased by 41.3 percent to .465, and goods imports as a share of sector GDP increased by 87 percent to .698.

If the time period is divided up, we can see in a bit more detail the changes in the composition of employment, across industries and over time. During the late 1970s and early 1980s, employment declined, often sharply, in many manufacturing industries. Several large, visible industries—notably apparel, machinery, and motor vehicles—sustained sizable employment losses, with declines of 11-17 percent (for the sector overall, employment fell by 8.5 percent from 1979 to 1985). A number of smaller industries, particularly in traditional heavy manufacturing, experienced significant percentage declines in employment: blast furnaces, −63.4 percent; iron and steel foundries, −53.2 percent; railroad locomotives, −81.4 percent; watches and clocks, −81.1 percent; and farm machinery and equipment, −62.5 percent.[1]

Very few industries saw employment rise, and for the most part, growing industries were not a part of traditional heavy manufacturing (printing and publishing, +18.6 percent; office and accounting machines, +26 percent; computers, +52 percent; and miscellaneous paper products, +10.8 percent). The average rate of job loss (calculated as the ratio of the number of workers permanently laid off to industry employment) was 5.6 percent, with a wide range, from some industries with low job-loss rates (beverages, 1.4 percent; paperboard, 2.0 percent; and drugs and pharmaceuticals, 2.1 percent) to other industries with high job loss rates (footwear, 10.9 percent; leather products, 10.1 percent; wood buildings and mobile homes, 12.3 percent; and farm machinery and equipment, 10.1 percent).

On the trade side, from 1979 to 1985 the strong dollar contributed to a 14 percent decline in import prices, and the market share of imports rose 4 percentage points on average (a 50 percent increase). Apparel, footwear, leather products, blast furnaces, engines and turbines, and toys all had increases in import share exceeding 10 percentage points. With the strong dollar, exports plunged, falling 25 percent on average. Textiles, apparel, and steel and metals all had export declines exceeding 50 percent. Leather products, apparel, and knitting mills all had a combination of the largest increases in import share and largest decreases in exports. Domestic demand was essentially flat, falling 1.6 percent, and it provided little relief to manufacturing from the combination of rising imports and falling exports.

Overall, conditions improved in manufacturing during the 1985-94 period, and then more steadily starting in 1995, as the economy strengthened. For the sector as a whole, employment fell 4.8 percent from 1985

---

1. Although the last three industries listed had dramatic percentage declines, they were not large-employment industries at the start of the period. Arithmetically, a given number divided by a small base produces a larger percentage change than the same number divided by a larger base.

to 1994 and rose a scant 0.1 percent from 1995 to 1999. A number of industries expanded employment, and just a few industries had large declines, notably electrical machinery and apparel. Employment continued to fall sharply in a number of smaller traditional import-competing industries (e.g., footwear, leather products, steel and metals, radio and television, and toys and sporting goods). Import prices rose from 1985 to 1994, and then declined in the late 1990s. The import share overall rose 4 percentage points (a 30 percent increase) by 1994.[2] There was strong domestic demand for manufactured goods, rising slowly from the economic expansion starting in 1993, and gaining strength through the end of the decade. From 1985 to 1994, exports surged across the board, with the falling dollar. Export growth was more restrained in the late 1990s, with a stronger dollar and weaker foreign demand.

From this overview of manufacturing during the past two decades, we turn to a summary of how changes in foreign competition, employment change, and job loss are related across and within manufacturing industries. This summary finishes setting the stage for an analysis of manufacturing jobs and workers.

Imports, Exports, Employment, and Job Loss

Cross-industry evidence shows that increasing imports are associated with employment reductions, whereas increasing exports (and domestic demand) enhance employment (Kletzer 2001). Within an industry, year to year, the employment-enhancing effects of expanding exports are significantly greater than the employment-reducing effects of increasing imports. Increasing foreign competition, measured as a decline in relative import price, is associated with a decline in employment (see also Revenga 1992).

These results, along with the vast majority of the research literature, use industry net employment change as the lens through which labor market effects are viewed (wages are also examined). This net change results from changes in the gross flows of new hires, recalls, quits, displacements, temporary layoffs, and retirements. Job displacement—permanent job loss—is the most visible of these events, and the one that most concerns workers, the general public, and policymakers.

Recent findings indicate that workers face a high risk of job loss in industries with a rising share of imports in domestic supply (first reported in Kletzer 1998a, and extended in Kletzer 2000 and 2001). There is a subset of industries—those with both high and increasing import shares, where the rate of job loss is high—that confront sustained import competition. Beyond this subset, the relationship between rising import share and high

---

2. As explained below, the industry import data run continuously through 1994.

rate of job loss is considerably weaker. This means that growing imports play a small role in job loss in the economy as a whole, but a large role in traditional import-competing industries. Within a given industry, more competitively priced imports (with falling relative import prices) are associated with job loss (see also Haveman 1998).

In sum, increasing imports and declining import prices are related to industry job loss. But this relationship is stronger in the subset of traditional import-competing industries than overall. Moreover, an open economy leads to more exports along with more imports, and these growing exports reduce job loss.[3] In short, some jobs are lost when imports rise, but other jobs are maintained or created when exports rise.

With our background discussion complete, we turn now to the primary task: defining trade-related job loss and understanding how workers who lose import-competing jobs adjust to their loss.

Defining Trade-Related Job Loss

"Trade-related job loss" is a familiar phrase with great political value. It is one of the prime suspects in the increased job insecurity reported by many American workers. It requires a clear, precise definition, one that is perhaps narrow but can be measured with available data.

As commonly understood and implemented in policy, trade-related job loss means job loss due to increasing imports, with little or no attention paid to the export side of trade. This import focus is unfortunate and unrealistic. Trade is more than imports. In fact, the link between exports and jobs is also widely recognized. Manufacturers of exports (and their workers) clearly understand the sensitivity of jobs to declining or sluggish export growth. In what follows, I do stay largely within the tradition of emphasizing imports, but I will discuss industry export activity when relevant.[4]

To isolate job loss related to increasing imports, most trade displacement studies have used the US Department of Labor's Trade Adjustment Assistance (TAA) administrative data because "increased imports" are one of several criteria used to certify displaced workers so that they will be eligible for adjustment assistance. For TAA (and NAFTA-TAA[5]) workers, certification establishes that the (former) firm experienced an increase in

---

3. A 10 percent increase in overall sales due to exports lowers the industry job loss rate by 2.2 percent (see Kletzer 2001).

4. Kletzer (2001) contains a more complete discussion of industry exports and job loss.

5. North American Free Trade Agreement-Transitional Adjustment Assistance is a NAFTA-specific TAA program.

imports.[6] TAA is first and foremost a program of targeted labor market assistance and not a means of *identifying* a representative group of import-displaced workers. Workers (and firms) must apply, and be eligible, for TAA. The application process is not transparent; unionized workers and workers in large firms are more likely to apply for and receive assistance.[7] These criteria raise selection questions; for example, workers who apply for program benefits may be those expecting difficult adjustments.

This book takes a different approach.[8] As an extension of the industry-level trade and job loss research reported here, a number of trade measures are used to classify industries by their degree of import competition. By applying this import-competition definition to the Displaced Worker Surveys (DWSs), supplements to the Current Population Survey (CPS), I offer an exhaustive three-way classification of all manufacturing industries by degree of import competition: high, medium, and low (described in detail below). Once an industry is classified as high import competing, all workers displaced from that industry are counted as "import-competing displaced," simply on the basis of the industry's high degree of import competition. The resulting sample is formally a sample of workers displaced from increasing import industries—initially, as if each and every job loss were caused by increasing imports.[9]

By focusing on the differences between import-displaced workers and other workers displaced from manufacturing (from less import-sensitive industries), I control, somewhat crudely and implicitly, for other sources of displacement, such as technological change or business-cycle variation. The remaining difference can be ascribed, with some confidence, to high import competition alone.[10]

---

6. Currently, the US Department of Labor TAA certification investigation focuses on whether (1) a significant number of workers have lost their jobs or are threatened with job loss, (2) the company's sales or production has decreased, and (3) imports of articles "like or directly competitive" have increased and "contributed importantly" to both the total or partial separation of workers and to the decline in sales or production (US General Accounting Office 2000). The importance of increased imports in TAA certification has varied somewhat over time. In the first years of TAA, eligibility criteria were quite strict, yielding few certifications. In the mid-1970s, much looser criteria greatly expanded the program.

7. Eligible petitioners include a group of three or more workers, a union (or other duly authorized representative), or a company official.

8. Kruse (1988) and Bednarzik (1993) are also exceptions in their use of non-TAA data.

9. The Bureau of International Labor Affairs (ILAB) of the US Department of Labor sponsored a number of empirical studies of trade-affected workers in the 1970s and early 1980s. See Aho and Orr (1979, 1981) and studies and citations in Dewald (1978).

10. If the import-competing industries face more intense foreign competition—and, from that competition, more technological advance—then my comparisons between import-competing displaced workers and workers displaced for other reasons will be less strongly due to increasing imports. In addition, workers in the less import-competing industries may also be displaced by import competition.

Measuring Imports, Exports, and Job Loss

This book focuses on import competition within the manufacturing sector for three reasons. First, historically, trade-flow data concentrated on goods (hence their name, merchandise trade statistics). Second, although trade now clearly involves services, data on them are much more limited. Third, public debate over "trade and jobs" very much concentrates on manufacturing.

Briefly, the trade-flow data were obtained from the National Bureau of Economic Research (NBER) Trade Database.[11] Data on imports, exports, and shipments are available for manufacturing industries defined at the detailed, 4-digit Standard Industrial Classification (SIC) level for the period 1958-94. The data on job displacement were obtained from the DWSs.[12] The industry classification scheme used by the CPS is the less detailed, 3-digit Census of Population Industrial Classification (CIC), which is used to report data on employment and job displacement. To bring together the two datasets thus required combining the SIC data at the CIC level. Because the DWS data are less well known, I will describe them briefly. (For the details on all data and sources, see appendix A.)

The Displaced Worker Survey is administered biennially as a supplement to the Current Population Survey. The first survey was done in January 1984 and the most recent in February 2000. The time series of surveys provides coverage of displacements during the period 1979-99. In each survey, adults (20 years and older) in the regular monthly CPS were asked if they had lost a job in the preceding 3- or 5-year period due to "a plant closing, an employer going out of business, a layoff from which he/she was not recalled, or other similar reasons."[13] If the answer was yes, a series of questions followed concerning the old job and period of joblessness. Other causes of job loss, such as quits or firings, are not considered displacements.[14] This categorization is consistent with our common understanding of job displacement: It occurs without personal prejudice, in that terminations are the result of the operating decisions of the employer and are independent of individual job performance.[15]

---

11. This dataset is described in Feenstra (1996) and can be obtained from the NBER Web site, http://www.nber.org.

12. Information about this publicly available dataset can be obtained from the US Department of Labor's Bureau of Labor Statistics Web site, http://stats.bls.gov.

13. For the 1984-92 surveys, the recall period was 5 years. Starting in 1994, the recall period was shortened to 3 years.

14. Individuals who respond that their job loss was due to the end of a seasonal job or the failure of a self-employed business are also not included.

15. There is some ambiguity: The displacements are "job" displacements, in the sense that an individual displaced from a job and rehired for a different job with the same employer is considered displaced.

A key advantage of the DWS is its large-scale, representative nature. As part of the CPS, it draws upon a random sample of 60,000 households, which is weighted to be representative of the US workforce. As a result, the surveys yield large numbers of displaced workers, from a large set of industries. In exchange for breadth of coverage, the DWSs suffer two weaknesses that are relevant here. First, they have a relatively short-term horizon. Individuals are surveyed just once, providing information on one postdisplacement point in time, rather than about their experiences over time. The second weakness is the lack of a readily available comparison group of nondisplaced workers. Without such a group, we cannot investigate what would have happened to these workers if they had not been displaced. The lack of a comparison group leads to some unavoidable errors in measuring outcomes, such as postdisplacement reemployment and earnings losses. I will discuss these errors where relevant. (Appendix A discusses data construction in more detail, and appendix C discusses displacement research using comparison groups.)

Defining an Import-Competing Industry

A widely accepted operational definition of an import-competing industry is one with a high import penetration rate (also called import share). In principle, this measure is not quite right, because it is changes in import share that are conceptually related to changes in employment (through changes in demand or sales), and job loss occurs from changes in employment. Empirically, industry-level studies establish changes in import share as one measure of changing import competition. The appropriateness of changes in import share also is highlighted by the language of Trade Adjustment Assistance, which makes certification for eligibility depend on an administrative determination that *increased* imports have contributed to worker layoffs.[16]

A set of high import-competing industries initially is defined here as those ranking in the top 25 percent in import share changes during the period 1979-94. This top quartile contains industries with an increase in import share exceeding 13 percentage points. With this cutoff as the primary criterion, I then adjust the group based on employment size and history of import competition.[17]

---

16. In practice, the two measures—level of import share and changes in import share—are highly correlated, and a classification of import-competing industries by one measure produces a list that is very similar to a list produced by the other measure.

17. Methodologically, some may claim that the conceptually correct way to measure import competition is to use changes in import prices and not changes in import quantities. This distinction is not at issue in this book. I discuss this point at some length in Kletzer (2001). I note here that for a large country such as the United States, import prices are also endogenous to forces determining production, employment, and job loss, and therefore changes in import prices are not clearly the conceptually correct choice.

Table 2.1 lists the high import-competing (or import-sensitive) industries. These industries are the most likely to produce an import-competing displaced worker, and workers displaced from these industries form the group of import-sensitive displaced workers.[18] Industries are defined and listed in table 2.1 at a 3-digit CIC level of detail.[19] For readability, some 3-digit industries are grouped together under more aggregated (or 2-digit) headings. Industries are listed in order of estimated total number of workers displaced during the period 1979-99, from largest to smallest. For each industry, from left to right, the table reports the total number of workers displaced, share of total manufacturing displaced, average job loss rate, change in import share, 1979 level of import share, and change in exports.[20] The last column, labeled "importer or exporter?," is a description of each industry's export as well as import intensity, and is explained in more detail below.

My judgments moved several industries into the high-import category: Motor vehicles, tires and inner tubes, blast furnaces, other primary metals, and cycles and miscellaneous transport all have a history of import competition, are large and visible employers, but experienced increases in import share just below the top quartile cutoff. One industry, aircraft and parts, was moved from the high-import to the medium-import group, despite its increase in import share, because it had little history of import competition (on the basis of a low level of import share in the mid-1970s).

Industries with smaller changes in import share and/or lower levels of import share are classified as "medium" and "low" import competing. Appendix table D.1 lists all manufacturing industries under this classification, with more detailed industry information. These medium and low industries will be used extensively in the analysis for comparison with the high-import group. By comparing the high-import group with the rest of manufacturing, I am implicitly controlling for other sectorwide structural economic changes within manufacturing that are associated with job loss, such as technological change, changes in consumer demand, and restructuring.

The high-import group contains the handful of industries commonly considered to be import competing: apparel, footwear, knitting mills, leather products, textiles, blast furnaces, radio and television, and toys and sporting goods. For the most part, these industries all faced considerable increases in import competition (all had increases in import share of at least 15 percentage points), and they have faced sustained import competition over time. In other words, these industries were in the top 25 percent on the basis of the average level of import share, and almost

---

18. The summary characteristics reported in table 2.1 (and conclusions) are robust to the subjective adjustments in the definition of "high import competing."

19. This means that an "industry" is a 3-digit CIC industry.

20. The change in exports is the change in log(exports).

all industries started the period with a high import share.[21] As noted above, some industries enter the group with high levels of import share without large increases in import share. Two industries stand out: motor vehicles and cycles and miscellaneous transport. Both industries had a high average level of import share during the period, but neither experienced a sizable increase in import share. Both industries received some protection from imports: In cycles, import restrictions in the 1980s were likely related to the measured fall in import share, and motor vehicles likely benefited from Japanese voluntary export restraints. Blast furnaces enters the group as an adjustment also, as a large employer with high average import share, but a mid-range increase in imports.

Table 2.1 reports an estimate of the total number of workers displaced from each industry during the period 1979-99. Details of the estimation method are discussed in appendix A. Some of the biggest increases in import share occurred in small-employment industries, such as watches and clocks, office and accounting machines, and leather products. Other traditional import-competing industries were associated with considerable displacement: apparel, electrical machinery, footwear, and radio and television.

Note that the high import-competing group contains many, if not most, of the usual suspects: footwear, apparel, leather products, and toys. The grouping also yields some surprises (or at least nuances): Most of the steel industry—here labeled metal industries—is in the medium import-competing group, with moderate increases in import share and a low initial import share. These industries are large employers, and some had considerable job loss, but not large increases in import share. Only blast furnaces and other primary metals are in the high import-competing group. Similarly, note that not all of textiles is included in the high import-competing group. Most textile job loss occurs from the industries in the medium import-competing group, due to the large size of the yarn and threads industry. The cases of metals and textiles—where job losses were extensive throughout the 2-digit industry, yet where import share increased in some but not all detailed (3-digit) industries—highlights the roles of other factors underlying job loss, including technological change.

The industry composition of NAFTA-TAA certifications provides a useful benchmark for the robustness of my criteria for import competition. Figure 2.1 reports the top 10 industries, in share of NAFTA-TAA certifications, as of August 2000.[22] Apparel, electrical machinery, and motor vehicles dominate in number of workers certified, just as they do in table 2.1

---

21. Schoepfle (1982) adopted a 15 percent import share cutoff as his definition of "import-sensitive." Bednarzik (1993) used a 30 percent import penetration ratio cutoff.

22. A searchable NAFTA-TAA database is available from Public Citizen at http://www.citizen.org/pcctrade/NAFTATAA.

Table 2.1 High import-competing industries and job displacement, 1979-99

High import-competing industry	Total displaced, 1979-99	Share of total manu-facturing displaced	Mean job loss rate	Change in import share			1979 import share (percent)	Change in exports, 1979-94 (percent)	Importer or exporter? Balanced or unbalanced?
				1979-94	1979-85	1985-94			
Electrical machinery, I	1,576,095								
Electrical machinery	1,180,706	0.0703	0.0402	0.2063	0.0712	0.1351	0.1066	1.1721	Balanced importer
Radio and television	395,389	0.0235	0.1052	0.147	0.0458	0.1012	0.151	1.312	Unbalanced importer
Apparel, I									
Apparel	1,135,668	0.0676	0.0562	0.2497	0.1034	0.1464	0.1322	1.3434	Unbalanced importer
Transportation equipment, I	985,760								
Motor vehicles	918,066	0.0546	0.0431	0.1012	0.0857	0.0156	0.1733	0.7828	Unbalanced importer
Cycles and miscellaneous transport	67,694	0.0040	0.0838	-0.0631	-0.0221	-0.041	0.2906	0.9753	Balanced importer
Machinery, except electrical, I	905,514								
Electronic computing equipment	513,988	0.0306	0.0454	0.384	0.086	0.298	0.1031	1.1805	Balanced exporter
Construction and material moving machines	350,900	0.0209	0.0526	0.1771	0.0905	0.0866	0.0595	-0.1908	Unbalanced exporter
Office and accounting machines	40,626	0.0024	0.0297	0.3715	0.0827	0.2888	0.0795	0.1494	Balanced importer
Metal industries, I	494,660								
Blast furnaces	361,428	0.0215	0.0531	0.0709	0.0739	-0.003	0.1191	0.017	Unbalanced importer
Other primary metals	133,232	0.0079	0.0719	0.0024	0.0222	-0.0198	0.189	-0.0474	Balanced importer

Miscellaneous manufacturing industries	335,091	0.0199	0.0505	0.1902	0.1099	0.0803	0.1857	0.0331	Unbalanced importer
Leather and leather products	246,451								
Footwear	184,417	0.0110	0.0871	0.3587	0.2192	0.1395	0.3478	1.3752	Unbalanced importer
Leather products	57,337	0.0034	0.1217	0.3906	0.195	0.1957	0.2694	0.7729	Unbalanced importer
Leather tanning and finishing	4,697	0.0003	0.074	0.1173	0.0725	0.0448	0.16	0.5605	Balanced exporter
Professional and photographic equipment	240,200								
Scientific and controlling instruments	163,503	0.0097	0.0278	0.154	0.0424	0.1116	0.0743	0.7092	Balanced exporter
Photographic equipment	67,754	0.0040	0.0321	0.1396	0.0519	0.0877	0.1206	0.0279	Balanced importer
Watches, clocks	8,943	0.0005	0.0913	0.4129	0.2261	0.1868	0.3873	−0.0476	Unbalanced importer
Rubber and miscellaneous plastics	192,960								
Other rubber products	113,144	0.0067	0.0437	0.1567	−0.0125	0.1692	0.0861	0.8918	Unbalanced importer
Tires and inner tubes	79,816	0.0048	0.0452	0.096	0.038	0.058	0.1295	1.0439	Unbalanced importer
Textiles, I	159,177								
Knitting mills	137,725	0.0082	0.0342	0.1585	0.0973	0.0612	0.0606	1.4413	Unbalanced importer
Miscellaneous textiles	21,452	0.0013	0.0449	0.0146	0.0142	0.0005	0.1186	0.7878	Balanced importer
Toys and sporting goods	155,970	0.0093	0.0597	0.2781	0.148	0.1301	0.2292	1.0191	Unbalanced importer
Pottery and related	26,471	0.0016	0.0733	0.1326	0.1054	0.0271	0.3126	0.7543	Unbalanced importer
Totals/means	6,454,017	0.3842	0.0594	0.1846	0.0846	0.1000	0.1689	0.6984	

Sources: Author's calculations from the National Bureau of Economic Research Trade Database and the Displaced Worker Surveys, 1984–2000.

Figure 2.1 Top 10 industries for NAFTA-TAA certifications, as of August 2000

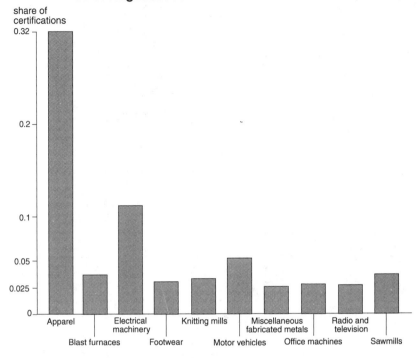

NAFTA-TAA = North American Free Trade Agreement-Transitional Adjustment Assistance.

Source: Author's calculations from Public Citizen's NAFTA-TAA database.

in accounting for the largest shares of manufacturing displaced. The only real difference between my set of import-competing industries and a NAFTA-TAA defined list is sawmills, which is on the NAFTA-TAA list due to Canadian imports. Sawmills is a medium import-competing industry in my categorization, and is listed in appendix table D.1.

Using the conservative count of displaced workers explained in appendix A, 16.8 million workers lost jobs in all of manufacturing during the period 1979-99, about 37 percent of the total nonagricultural job loss of 44.9 million.[23] Yet during this period, manufacturing represented, typically, about 18 percent of total nonagricultural employment (23.4 percent in 1979, 16.0 percent in 1994, and 14.3 percent in 1999). It is clear that

---

23. This number will be different from the often-cited declines in employment in manufacturing. Manufacturing employment decline is a net loss in employment, the difference between employment gains (through new hires, rehires, and recalls) and reductions in employment (through quits, layoffs, displacements, retirements, and deaths).

manufacturing workers are overrepresented among displaced workers, relative to their employment share. To get a perspective on the scale of job loss and employment decline in manufacturing, nearly as many workers lost manufacturing jobs during 1979-99 (16.8 million) as were employed in manufacturing in 1999 (18.5 million). Employment in manufacturing has traditionally been more sensitive to business cycle fluctuations than employment in utilities, wholesale and retail trade, and services.[24]

The high import-competing group accounted for 38.4 percent of manufacturing displacement, at 6.45 million workers. Yet during the period 1979-99, these industries accounted for just under 30 percent of manufacturing employment. Thus import-competing industries account for a greater share of job loss than their share of employment. We can see this quite clearly when we compare the high import-competing group with the total (nonagricultural) labor force. Averaged over the period 1979-94, the high import-competing manufacturing industries accounted for 5.2 percent of total nonagricultural employment. By my measure, job losses from these industries accounted for 14.2 percent of nonagricultural displacement.

A bit of additional perspective on the size of these job loss numbers can be gained by considering, briefly, other measures of US labor market turnover. The US labor market is characterized by substantial turnover, even when overall employment is stable. Flows in and out of jobs, employment creation and destruction, are all sizable. Two examples: for 2000, the average monthly gain in payroll employment was 219,000 jobs. And in April 2001, as the economy slowed down, payroll employment fell by 223,000. From a point of overall labor market strength to one of weakening, we can see the swings are reversed, with similar magnitude.

By any measure, there is a lot of job loss in the US economy, even in good times. In 1999, with an average unemployment rate of 4.2 percent, 2.5 million workers lost their jobs. From its Mass Layoffs Statistics (MLS) program, the Bureau of Labor Statistics reported 120,370 nonseasonal extended mass layoffs for the second quarter of 2000.[25] At this same rate, on a yearly basis, there would have been 481,480 layoffs. Using a less restrictive definition of job loss, in the most recent DWS (February 2000), 7.6 million workers, from all levels of job tenure, reported a job loss between January 1997 and December 1999. On a yearly basis, that would

---

24. This difference narrowed in the 1990s, as compared with the 1980s. Throughout, however, job loss rates in manufacturing show a countercyclical pattern, rising in recessions and falling during recoveries (see Kletzer 2000). For an extended discussion of job loss over time, see Farber (1997, 2001).

25. Nonseasonal layoffs exclude those due to the end of seasonal work (primarily in food production), extended layoffs last more than 30 days, and mass layoffs involve 50 workers or more from an establishment.

be about 2.5 million displaced workers. During the 21-year period of this sample, 6.45 million workers lost jobs in import-competing industries; that is 307,142 workers per year.

There is notably less manufacturing displacement now than was the case from the late 1970s to the mid-1990s. Manufacturing displacement during the period 1997-99 affected 1 million workers, or 333,333 a year, less than the 1979-94 manufacturing annual average of 750,000 workers.

Because a few import-competing industries are large employers, there is some further concentration, by industry, in import-competing displacement. Three industries, electrical machinery, apparel, and motor vehicles, accounted for 19 percent of manufacturing displacement. At the beginning of the period, they accounted for 17 percent of manufacturing employment. The top five, adding electronic computing equipment (computers) and blast furnaces, accounted for just under 25 percent of displacement, and 22 percent of 1979 employment. These industries all had high and rising import shares during the period.[26]

Is the risk of job loss higher in import-competing industries? Not clearly so, using a measure of the likelihood of job loss—the job loss rate—reported in table 2.1. An annual job loss rate for an industry is the ratio of the number of workers displaced to average employment. Table 2.1 reports a mean job loss rate for each industry. The mean job loss rate for 1979-99 was 5.9 percent of employment in the high import-competing group, relative to 6.2 percent in the medium group and 4.2 percent in the low group.[27] So there was a higher risk of job loss in the most import-sensitive industries, in comparison with the least import-sensitive (or more insular), but a similar risk of job loss in the set of industries less sensitive to rising imports. This reveals that the link between job loss and rising import share is complicated: some of the industries with high job loss had large increases in import share (e.g., leather products, pottery and related products, and radio and television), but within and across industries, the relationship between rising import share and the risk of job loss is considerably weaker.

Exports and Import-Competing Industries

As was noted above, the traditional discussions of the "costs of trade," both academic and in policy circles, focus almost singularly on imports. Trade, of course, includes both imports and exports, and many industries, including our high-import industries, do both. The simple view of trade—that the

---

26. For a detailed analysis of industry changes in import share (and exports) over this time period, see Kletzer (2000).

27. The group (high, medium, low) mean job loss rate was calculated by weighting each industry mean by beginning-period industry employment.

United States imports watches and apparel and exports airplanes and bulldozers—is wrong. A more realistic view is that the United States imports and exports all four of these goods, as either intermediate or final goods.

Up to this point, our discussion considers industries as "importers," but it is important to note that three of the top five US export industries in 1994 are members of our import-competing group: electrical machinery and equipment (accounting for 11.4 percent of total manufacturing exports); motor vehicles (10.8 percent); and electronic computing equipment (7.0 percent). The remaining two industries are medium import-competing: aircraft and parts (8.3 percent) and nonelectrical machinery (5.8 percent).

More generally, to varying degrees, our import-competing industries are engaged in two-way trade, with flows of exports as well as imports.[28] We have seen so far that all the industries in the high-import group faced increased competition from imports since 1979. Allowing for two-way trade allows us to see that, to some degree, these same industries were engaged in production for foreign markets.

An established method for measuring the degree of intraindustry trade (or trade overlap) is available from a method first presented in Grubel and Lloyd (1975). Appendix B describes a simple version of the Grubel-Lloyd trade overlap index. In this version, the value of the index ranges from 0, when an industry only exports or imports but does not do both, to 1, when an industry's exports and imports are equal. The higher the value of the index, the greater the degree of trade overlap, or intraindustry trade. Restated, we can think of balanced industries as those with a high degree of trade overlap, where flows of exports and imports are equal or nearly so. Unbalanced industries are those where one of the flows dominates the other in size.

A simple alteration of the Grubel-Lloyd measure, using positive or negative net exports, reveals not only whether trade is balanced, but also whether an industry is relatively more export oriented or import oriented. With this alteration, I can make a straightforward judgment as to whether an industry is an exporter or importer, balanced or unbalanced. My revised Grubel-Lloyd index yields values near 0 for unbalanced exporters, values closer to 1 (but less than 1) for balanced exporters, values close to 1 (but greater than 1) for balanced importers, and the largest values for unbalanced importers (see appendix B for more details).

My own characterization of an industry's level of engagement in world trade (balanced or unbalanced) and direction (exporter or importer) is

---

28. An extensive literature explains and measures within-industry, or intraindustry, trade (see Kletzer 2001 for a summary). Lovely and Richardson (2000) present a useful characterization of intraindustry trade. Between industrial countries (North-North), trade flows within an industry are differentiated as skill-intensive intermediate or final goods. Between industrial and newly industrialized countries (North-South), the North exports skill-intensive intermediate or final goods, and the South exports labor-intensive intermediates. Southern production of labor-intensive intermediates (or the labor-intensive assembly component of final goods) is also known as Northern "outsourcing," the import of intermediate inputs.

reported in the last column of table 2.1 for the high import-competing industries. The indices themselves are reported in the more detailed appendix table D.1.[29] Nineteen of 23 industries in this group are importers, with 13 (56 percent) unbalanced importers. These unbalanced importers import far more than they export. This is what we expect from this group. These industries (among them apparel, motor vehicles, blast furnaces, radio and television, footwear, toys and sporting goods, knitting mills, leather products, and watches and clocks) are perhaps the most strongly associated with import competition. It is perhaps notable that of the industries listed in table 2.1 that are "traditional import competing" (in the sense of being the industries long identified as import sensitive), all are unbalanced importers.[30] The balanced industries are the next set, with six importers and three exporters. Trade flows are more balanced in durable goods than in nondurable goods. Two industries with some of the largest increases in import share are, upon reflection, more balanced trade industries (electronic computing equipment and office and accounting machines). In each of these industries, both exports and imports rose strongly, with exports dominating in electronic computing equipment, and imports in office and accounting machines.

There is considerable balanced trade in leather tanning and finishing, miscellaneous textile mill products, machinery, farm equipment, and cycles and miscellaneous transport, where high import share is combined with high export intensity. These industries again face significant import competition but are also highly engaged in exporting. There is only one industry that I call an "unbalanced exporter," construction and material moving machines. This industry started from a low level of import competition, experienced a sizable (17 percentage points) increase in import share, and saw its high level of exports decline during the 1979-94 period (by 19 percent). When the dollar was strong during the 1979-85 period, this industry was vulnerable to both rising imports and declining exports. As a large-employment industry with an above-average job loss rate, it contributed notably to manufacturing job loss.

Appendix table D.1 reports on the full set of manufacturing industries. A few observations: In the medium-import group, where we might expect a more balanced engagement with the world, we see just that: 32 percent are unbalanced importers; 59 percent are balanced, tilted either toward

---

29. At the level of aggregation in this dataset, it is not surprising that industries are both importers and exporters. For example, in motor vehicles (defined here as CIC 351), where finished cars are included with parts, firms located in the United States import parts for US production (Honda; Toyota; the NUMMI plant in Fremont, CA), and parts are exported for Canadian production. Of course, finished cars are imported and exported.

30. See Schoepfle (1982) for a list of import-sensitive industries using data from the 1970s. His methodology for classifying industries is similar (although he uses 4-digit SIC industry codes), and the resulting industry list is very similar.

imports or exports; and 11 percent are unbalanced exporters. The low-import group contains industries that tend to be domestically oriented, with little import or export activity, along with industries that actively export. Industries balanced with very little trade (high domestic orientation) include dairy products; bakery products; paperboard containers; printing and publishing; cement, concrete, and gypsum; and fabricated structural metal. This group also includes the unbalanced and high-export industries: logging, tobacco, grain mill products.

Note that not all the industries listed in table 2.1 are unbalanced importers. Although the list is generated from changes in import share, which makes sense from a job loss perspective, a rapid or large rise in import share need not necessarily mean a loss of competitiveness. As indicated by the balanced importers and exporters, a rise in imports, accompanied by a rise in exports, may signal intraindustry trade and/or product specialization. In addition, the fact that high import-competing industries are not just unbalanced importers indicates the dynamic notion of import competition.

Exports and imports have increased over time in many industries. Even where there is far more trade in one direction than the other (unbalanced trade), the smaller of the flows increased during the study period. Sixty percent of manufacturing industries were more balanced in trade by 1994 than in 1979 or in comparison with the average measure reported in appendix table D.1. Exports represent a small, although far from trivial, share of domestic shipments in traditional import-competing industries, such as footwear, watches and clocks, leather products, pottery, and toys and sporting goods. Other traditional import-competing industries have more balanced trade, such as leather tanning and finishing, cycles and miscellaneous transport. Yet the direction of future trade orientation of these industries is unclear, because 13 of the 23 high import-competing industries became less balanced (increased their degree of unbalanced importing) during the period.

We can draw out some relationships between job loss and an industry's trade orientation. Unbalanced importers dominate the group of high import-competing industries (13 of 23, or 56 percent). These industries account for 60.5 percent of the group's total job losses (3,909,465 workers), whereas they accounted for 55 percent of beginning employment. Seven of these 13 industries have job loss rates higher than the manufacturing average, and the 3 industries with the highest job loss rates are all unbalanced importers. The 6 balanced importers accounted for 21.3 percent of group job losses (1,378,232 workers), from a 26 percent beginning-employment share. Just 2, or a third, of these industries had average job loss rates higher than the manufacturing average. The numbers of exporters are a bit smaller, making summary statistics more tenuous. The 3 balanced exporters produced 682,188 job losses, 10.5 percent of the group total. One industry, leather tanning and finishing, had an above-average job loss rate. Together, the 9 balanced industries accounted for 31.8 percent of group job losses and 36 percent of employment. Some of the industries with the lowest job loss rates are balanced-trade industries. On balance, this accounting shows that the risk of job loss is greater in unbalanced importers and that these industries produce a slightly greater share of job loss than employment. This is consistent with earlier statements noting the greater risk of job loss from industries with a high, rising import share. These industries are the unbalanced importers. More balanced-trade industries have less job loss and a lower risk of loss.

Beyond offering a more realistic view of these manufacturing industries, including exports in our trade picture allows job loss to be mitigated by increasing exports or increased by falling exports. American jobs are not just vulnerable to rising imports; they are vulnerable to falling exports. This point is not missed by those decrying the large US trade deficit.[31] From this appraisal of industry trade engagement and trends in job loss, we turn to the workers: who they are and how they adjust to job displacement.

---

31. For an interesting set of discussions, see the Web site and final report of the US Trade Deficit Review Commission, http://www.ustdrc.gov.

3

Who Are Import-Competing Displaced Workers?

This chapter examines the characteristics of import-competing displaced workers, comparing them with other manufacturing workers and with workers displaced from other sectors of the economy. This comparison provides an opportunity to explain the differences between manufacturing workers and other, nonmanufacturing workers, and—more important to the task at hand—the differences between import-competing displaced workers and manufacturing workers displaced for other reasons. Explaining the individual and labor market characteristics of this group of displaced workers is an important first step in explaining the consequences of their job loss.

One focus of the examination will be to consider the realism of the common perception that import-competing displaced workers are unskilled. Sachs and Shatz provide just one example of this view when they write "that a cutback in manufacturing employment (particularly import-competing manufacturing employment) will release relatively unskilled workers into the service sector, with the effect being larger should those employees come from the import-competing sector of manufacturing" (1998, 30).

The sample used in this chapter and those that follow differ very slightly from the one used in chapter 2. One goal for chapter 2 was to establish a reliable, if conservative, count of the number of displaced workers (taking into account the recall-period limitations discussed in appendix A). With this point established, it is desirable to use the fullest possible representation of displaced workers, so as to explain more fully the individual and labor market characteristics of affected workers. To accomplish this goal, I ignore differential recall periods and include all workers displaced from the relevant industries in all years of the surveys.

Comparing Manufacturing with Nonmanufacturing Workers

Table 3.1 reports basic individual characteristics for two subsets of the sample, manufacturing and nonmanufacturing workers, for the period 1979-99. The group of nonmanufacturing workers includes those displaced from transportation, utilities, communications, wholesale and retail trade, finance, insurance, real estate, and services. Throughout this analysis, workers displaced from agriculture, mining, and construction are excluded. Averages are calculated across workers, not from industry means. (A full set of tables, with separate panels for various time periods, is given in appendix table D.2.)

There is one very important first observation from table 3.1: manufacturing displaced workers are different from nonmanufacturing ones. Manufacturing displaced workers are older, less educated, notably more tenured, considerably less likely to be female, more likely to be minority, and far more likely to be production oriented (in particular, lower-skill production oriented) than nonmanufacturing ones. These differences have been maintained during the 21 years of the sample (see panels A-C of appendix table D.2).

The education, tenure, and occupation differences are particularly stark. Twenty-one percent of manufacturing displaced workers are high school dropouts, relative to 11.9 percent of nonmanufacturing ones. This difference widened in the 1990s as compared with the 1980s: the share dropped throughout the economy, but more so outside manufacturing. The share of manufacturing workers who were high school dropouts was 60 percent higher than the nonmanufacturing share for the period 1979-89, and the share of manufacturing workers who were high school dropouts was 80 percent higher than the nonmanufacturing share for 1990-99. Similarly, manufacturing workers are less likely to be college graduates: during the 1979-99 period, workers with a college degree or higher made up about 14 percent of the manufacturing displaced and 22 percent of the nonmanufacturing displaced. This difference remained constant during the 21-year period.

In the displacement literature, there is a clear focus on workers with established work histories, for whom some of the risks of job loss seem clear. Human capital (skills) specific to firms and employers may be lost, job search skills are rusty, and starting over may be difficult. In regard to job tenure, manufacturing workers are far more likely to have long tenure: during the 1979-99 period, 21.5 percent of manufacturing displaced workers had more than 10 years' tenure on their lost job, as com-

Table 3.1 Characteristics of displaced manufacturing and nonmanufacturing workers, 1979-99

Worker characteristics	Manu-facturing (share)	Nonmanu-facturing (share)
Age at displacement (years)		
20-24	0.144	0.164
25-34	0.333	0.344
35-44	0.254	0.256
45-54	0.168	.153
55-64	0.101	0.082
Mean age, years (standard deviation)	38.6	37.3
	(11.5)	(11.2)
Education		
Less than high school	0.210	0.119
High school graduate	0.437	0.365
Some college	0.215	0.294
College degree or higher	0.137	0.222
Mean years of education (standard deviation)	12.3	13.2
	(2.6)	(2.4)
Job tenure at time of displacement (years)		
Less than 3	0.402	0.510
3-5	0.227	0.229
6-10	0.156	0.133
11-20	0.131	0.082
Greater than 20	0.084	0.045
Mean job tenure, years (standard deviation)	6.5	4.6
	(7.8)	(6.2)
Share female	0.369	0.504
Share minority	0.176	0.170
Share displaced from full-time jobs	0.956	0.837
Predisplacement occupation		
White collar	0.307	0.645
Skilled blue collar	0.188	0.075
Unskilled blue collar	0.480	0.138
Services	0.023	0.140
Weekly earnings on old job		
Mean (standard deviation)	$396.88	$368.65
	($250.89)	($269.19)
Share earned less than $200/week	0.18	0.28
Share earned more than $800/week	0.06	0.07
Share reemployed at survey date	0.648	0.691
For reemployed workers		
Mean change in log earnings (standard deviation)	−0.121	−0.038
	(0.473)	(0.575)
Median change in log earnings	−0.047	0
Share with no earnings loss or earning more	0.35	0.41
Share with earnings losses greater than 15 percent	0.35	0.29
Share with earnings losses greater than 30 percent	0.25	0.21

Note: Workers displaced from agriculture, mining, construction, forestry, and fishing were excluded.

Source: Author's calculations from the Displaced Worker Surveys, 1984-2000, using sampling weights.

pared with 12.7 percent of nonmanufacturing ones. On the other side of the tenure distribution, there is a different story, one contrary to expectations. Many displaced workers do not have particularly long job tenure. Forty percent of manufacturing workers and 51 percent of nonmanufacturing workers were displaced after fewer than 3 years on the job.[1]

Previewing what lies ahead, job tenure is an important characteristic for explaining (and predicting) difficult labor market adjustments. Long-tenured workers are less likely to be reemployed, and once reemployed, they experience larger earnings losses. For workers with shorter work histories before job loss, there may still be losses, in particular the earnings growth that would have been realized if the old job had not ended.[2] This second type of earnings loss is difficult to measure in the Displaced Worker Surveys.

In regard to occupation, just less than half (48 percent) of the manufacturing displaced are lower-skilled blue collar workers (fabricators, laborers, et al.), as compared with 14 percent of the nonmanufacturing displaced. There is a countertrend, appearing over time. The share of white collar workers among the manufacturing displaced rose sharply, from 27.9 percent for the period 1979-89 to 35.3 percent for 1990-99. This is consistent with the increase in the share of displaced workers with some college experience, from 29.9 percent for 1979-89 to 43.8 percent for 1990-99.[3] The risks of job loss have clearly changed in manufacturing, spreading throughout the sector from production workers to nonproduction workers. This change put more-educated workers at greater risk of job loss by the late 1990s than they were in the 1980s.

Earnings on the old job were higher for the average manufacturing worker than for the average nonmanufacturing one.[4] The difference (statistically significant at the mean) was about 8 percent and fairly constant over time. The earnings difference at the median, about 15 percent, was considerably greater, due to the larger share of nonmanufacturing workers earning less than $200 a week. During the full period, 1979-99, fully 28 percent of nonmanufacturing workers earned less than $200 a week, as compared with 18 percent of manufacturing ones. Part of this difference in the incidence of low earnings is accounted for by the difference in the prevalence of full-time work. Ninety-five percent of displaced manufac-

---

1. This is consistent with more general reports from the Displaced Worker Surveys. About half of all displaced workers have less than 3 years' tenure on the old job. See Hipple (1999).

2. In an analysis of displacement among young adult workers, Kletzer and Fairlie (2001) report sizable earnings losses for young job losers, relative to what they would have earned if not displaced.

3. See Kletzer (1995b) for a broader discussion of white collar job loss.

4. Earnings are reported in 1987 dollars.

turing workers reported being on the old job full time; about 84 percent of nonmanufacturing workers reported the same.[5]

The analysis below examines how these differences matter for postdisplacement outcomes and consequences. At this point, I note that a widely recognized finding from the displaced-worker literature (particularly on those displaced by trade) is that workers who are older, less educated, and longer tenured have more difficult and costly adjustments to permanent job loss.[6]

Outcomes after Job Loss

Turning from characteristics to consequences, the first postdisplacement outcome of interest is reemployment—becoming employed again in a new job. On this score, manufacturing workers do not fare as well as nonmanufacturing ones. This difference in outcomes can be seen in the lower half of table 3.1, where the share of workers reemployed is reported. In the Displaced Worker Surveys, reemployment is measured as survey date reemployment.[7] About 65 percent of manufacturing displaced workers were reemployed at their survey date, as compared with 69 percent of nonmanufacturing ones. (This difference, 4.3 percentage points, is not large, but it is statistically significant at the 1 percent level.)

The likelihood of reemployment was markedly higher in the 1990s than in the 1980s. During the period 1990-99, the manufacturing reemployment rate was 66.3 percent, 2.3 percentage points higher than it was for 1979-89. For nonmanufacturing, the strong labor market of the late 1990s provided an even bigger boost: reemployment rose to a 70.8 percent average for the 1990s, 3.8 points higher than its 1980s average. This is consistent with the far more robust employment growth of services in the 1990s, relative to manufacturing. It is notable that it took the robustly strong labor market of the late 1990s for the manufacturing reemployment rate to equal the nonmanufacturing reemployment rate of the more troubled 1980s.

Earnings on the new job are the next concern—in particular, how earnings on the new job compare with earnings on the old one. Earnings are measured in the Displaced Worker Surveys as weekly earnings, and the

---

5. For the nonmanufacturing workers displaced from full-time jobs during the period 1979-99, mean weekly earnings on the old job were $400 a week, with 20 percent earning less than $200 a week and 8 percent earning more than $800 a week. This earnings distribution is similar to the manufacturing-worker distribution.

6. For an early reference, see Neumann (1978).

7. This measure could understate total reemployment because it misses spells of employment that begin and end before the date on which a worker is surveyed. Workers not employed at their survey date may also become reemployed in the future.

available comparison is between weekly earnings at the time of displacement and, if reemployed, weekly earnings at the time of the survey. In other words, earnings losses are measured as old job to new job. This measure will "miss" earnings growth that would have occurred on the old job, in the absence of displacement.[8] Manufacturing displaced workers experience large earnings losses on average, 12 percent at the mean, in comparison with a loss of just under 4 percent for nonmanufacturing ones.[9] This average masks considerable heterogeneity, and the real story lies in the distribution. Half of those displaced from manufacturing have earnings losses greater than 5 percent, as compared with the median nonmanufacturing earnings change of 0 percent. Approximately 25 percent of manufacturing workers report earnings losses of 30 percent or more, and 35 percent report earning the same or more on their postdisplacement job than on their predisplacement one. For nonmanufacturing displaced workers, the share with very large (30 percent or more) earnings losses is slightly smaller (21 percent), and the share of workers with no earnings loss or an earnings gain is 41 percent.[10] In contrast to differences over time in reemployment rates, the manufacturing-nonmanufacturing difference in earnings changes remained relatively unchanged from the 1980s to the 1990s.

Earnings losses exceeding 30 percent are very costly. Within the framework of Trade Adjustment Assistance, the mandate is to assist individuals who become unemployed as a result of foreign imports to return to suitable employment as quickly as possible. Suitable employment is defined as work that is substantially equal to—or higher in skill level than—the person's past adversely affected employment, and that pays not less than 80 percent of his or her previous employment.[11] The more detailed panels of appendix table D.2 show that the risk to workers of experiencing very large earnings losses is insensitive to business cycle and labor market fluctuations.

---

8. For some groups of workers, earnings fall before displacement, and the DWSs also miss this aspect of displacement-related earnings change (see Jacobson, LaLonde, and Sullivan 1993; Stevens 1997).

9. Very low reemployment earnings can dramatically increase estimates of earnings losses. To minimize the role of these outliers, workers with reemployment earnings below $75 a week (about 1.5 percent of reemployed workers) were omitted.

10. An important weakness of the DWS is the lack of a control group. The proper measure of earnings loss is not the comparison between pre- and postdisplacement earnings; rather, it is the difference in earnings between observationally similar displaced and nondisplaced workers. See Ruhm (1991) and Jacobson, LaLonde, and Sullivan (1993) for two different displaced-worker studies using control groups.

11. See the discussion of Trade Act programs at the US Department of Labor Web site, http://wdsc.doleta.gov/trade_act/.

These losses, although sizable, underestimate total earnings losses, if those losses are defined with respect to what workers would have earned if they had not been displaced. If these workers had not been displaced, they would have realized at least some earnings growth. Longitudinal studies, which follow a group of individuals over time, offer the best information for constructing a comparison group of nondisplaced workers. These studies are discussed in appendix C. For a sample of long-tenured Pennsylvania workers displaced in the 1980s, Jacobson, LaLonde, and Sullivan (1993) found that earnings fall dramatically below the levels expected in the absence of displacement. In the first year after job loss, earnings losses calculated this way averaged 40 percent of predisplacement earnings. Even during the fifth year after job separation, earnings losses averaged 25 percent of former earnings.[12]

Even at this summary level, the distribution of earnings losses has clear implications for US worker adjustment assistance policy and for our understanding of who most needs assistance. One-third of workers (and more for nonmanufacturing ones) experience no earnings loss or even a gain in pay with reemployment. For these workers, job displacement does not result in a diminished ability to support themselves and their families.[13] To meet the most immediate needs, resources can be targeted to those workers facing much more costly adjustments, those with earnings losses. About 30 percent of manufacturing workers face earnings losses of 0-15 percent, and a quarter of manufacturing workers experience very large earnings losses. With many workers experiencing small or zero earnings losses, the costs of a simple program of financial assistance, conditioned on earnings losses upon reemployment, are quite reasonable. Adjustment policies are discussed in chapter 7.

Comparing Import-Competing Displaced Workers with Other Manufacturing Workers

What about import-competing displaced workers? Using my import-competition categories, table 3.2 reports basic worker characteristics for high, medium, and low import-competing manufacturing industries. There is (again) one clear first observation: The average import-competing displaced worker looks very much like any other manufacturing worker.

---

12. Farber (2001) offers a method for calculating a similar control group from the Current Population Surveys. Overall, he reports that accounting for lost earnings growth can increase the estimate of earnings losses considerably, by about 50 percent in the 1980s. In the early 1990s, particularly for less-educated workers, the underestimate is smaller, because there was virtually no earnings growth. The general rise in real wages from 1995 increases estimates of total earnings loss, to the extent that most of the loss is forgone earnings growth.

13. This statement takes earnings as a primary component of compensation.

Table 3.2 Characteristics of displaced workers, by manufacturing-industry level of import competition, 1979-99

Worker characteristics	High import competition (share)	Medium import competition (share)	Low import competition (share)
Age at displacement (years)			
20-24	0.131	0.149	0.157
25-34	0.323	0.338	0.340
35-44	0.267	0.240	0.262
45-54	0.174	0.169	0.155
55-64	0.104	0.103	0.087
Mean age (standard	39.1	38.4	37.8
deviation)	(11.4)	(11.6)	(11.3)
Education			
Less than high school	0.213	0.219	0.182
High school graduate	0.427	0.444	0.446
Some college	0.212	0.210	0.229
College degree or higher	0.148	0.126	0.142
Mean years of education	12.3	12.3	12.5
(standard deviation)	(2.7)	(2.6)	(2.5)
Job tenure at time of displacement (years)			
Less than 3	0.388	0.398	0.442
3-5	0.221	0.231	0.230
6-10	0.168	0.154	0.134
11-20	0.130	0.133	0.125
Greater than 20	0.091	0.083	0.069
Mean job tenure, years	6.8	6.5	5.9
(standard deviation)	(7.9)	(7.8)	(7.7)
Share female	0.449	0.304	0.351
Share minority	0.190	0.165	0.167
Share displaced from full-time jobs	0.966	0.960	0.924
Predisplacement occupation			
White collar	0.313	0.286	0.345
Skilled blue collar	0.180	0.209	0.155
Unskilled blue collar	0.488	0.478	0.466
Services	0.018	0.025	0.029
Weekly earnings on the old job			
Mean (standard deviation)	$402.97	$400.41	$375.11
	($273.39)	($236.55)	($230.52)
Share earned less than $200/week	0.24	0.16	0.18
Share earned more than $800/week	0.07	0.06	0.05

Source: Author's calculations from the Displaced Worker Surveys, 1984-2000, using sampling weights.

Import-competing workers are very slightly older (a larger share are 45-54 years of age), their educational levels are very similar, and they have similar average levels of job tenure. Those displaced from high import-competing industries do have slightly more job tenure than those displaced from industries with less import competition, with most of the difference occurring at less than 3 years' tenure.[14] The most striking characteristic is the degree to which high import-competing industries employ and displace women. This difference was sharper in the 1990s than in the 1980s. Import-competing industries account for a large share of female employment in manufacturing.[15] This concentration of female manufacturing employment puts women at a relatively higher risk of import-competing job loss. This concentration is reflected in table 3.2, where women represent 45 percent of those displaced from high import-competing industries, 30 percent from medium, and 35 percent from low. These differences are all statistically significant, and they arise from the far greater level of female employment in traditional import-competing industries. This predominance is examined in more detail below.

High- and low-wage industries are fairly evenly represented among the import-competing displaced. For high and medium import-competing industry workers, mean real predisplacement weekly earnings are very similar, and somewhat higher than the least import-competing of the manufacturing industries (the high-low and medium-low differences are statistically significant). As we will see below, these averages (again) mask considerable variation. There are a number of low-wage traditional import-competing industries, and workers in them are observably different from workers in the rest of manufacturing.

Turning to postdisplacement outcomes in table 3.3, high import-competing displaced workers are less likely to be reemployed than other displaced manufacturing workers, with an average rate for 1979-99 of 63.4 percent. The difference between high and low import-competing workers, 3.4 percentage points, is statistically significant. The high-medium difference is smaller, at 2 points, also statistically significant. The medium-low difference is small, at 1.4 percentage points, and is not statistically significant.

Particularly for the high import-competing group, reemployment was more difficult in the 1980s, with a lower rate of 62.3 percent, than it was

---

14. The high, medium, and low distinctions made in this section are robust to alterations in the definition of import competing.

15. At the beginning of the study period, 1978, industries with an average import share of 0.20 or higher accounted for 6.8 percent of female manufacturing employment, relative to 2.6 percent of male manufacturing employment. Industries with the smallest exposure to imports, those with an average import share of less than 0.10, respectively accounted for 53.4 and 66.9 percent of female and male manufacturing employment (see Kletzer 1995a).

Table 3.3 Postdisplacement outcomes, by manufacturing-industry level of import competition, 1979-99

Outcomes	High import competition (share)	Medium import competition (share)	Low import competition (share)
Share reemployed at survey date	0.634	0.654	0.668
For reemployed:			
Mean change in log earnings	−0.132	−0.126	−0.086
(standard deviation)	(0.475)	(0.469)	(0.475)
Median change in log earnings	−0.047	−0.062	−0.027
Share with no earnings loss or earning more	0.36	0.34	0.38
Share with earnings losses greater than 15 percent	0.35	0.36	0.34
Share with earnings losses greater than 30 percent	0.25	0.25	0.26

Source: Author's calculations from the Displaced Worker Surveys, 1984-2000, using sampling weights.

in the 1990s, when 65.4 percent of workers were reemployed, on average (see appendix table D.2). Reemployment differences between the 1980s and 1990s were smaller for other displaced manufacturing workers.

Among the reemployed, high import-competing displaced workers have large average earnings losses, about 13 percent at the mean. This average earnings loss is significantly different from workers displaced from industries with the least exposure to imports, but not the medium-import group. Again, these large average losses mask considerable heterogeneity: 36 percent of import-competing displaced workers report earning the same or more after displacement as before, and 25 percent reported losses of 30 percent or more. This spread is very similar to manufacturing as a whole.

Drawing these elements together, there are few striking differences between import-competing displaced workers and other manufacturing workers, on the basis of average characteristics. It is useful, however, to look beyond the averages and at the distribution of these characteristics. Table 3.4 reports on a set of characteristics (expanded from tables 3.2 and 3.3) for just the high-import group of industries and workers. Appendix tables D.3 and D.4 report similarly for medium and low import-competing industries.

High import-competing industries vary from the low wage (apparel, footwear, knitting mills, and leather products) to the high wage (computers, blast furnaces, tires and inner tubes, construction and material moving machines, and motor vehicles). Note that the low-wage industries tend to be unbalanced importers, and the high-wage ones balanced or even unbalanced exporters. This is consistent with studies that reveal that exporting plants and firms offer "better" jobs, with higher pay and more job security (see Richardson and Rindal 1995, 1996).

Across the board, the low-wage industries employ and displace large shares (and often large numbers) of women. A few industries stand out: Women account for 79 percent of displaced workers from apparel (compared with their 82 percent employment share in 1978). In footwear, women represent 66 percent of displaced workers, from a 70 percent 1978 employment share. In leather products, women are 73 percent of the displaced, and 69 percent of 1978 employment. From knitting mills, women account for 80 (!) percent of displaced workers. The large shares of women in the groups of displaced workers, relative to their employment shares, may not be an overrepresentation due solely to gender. Shorter average job tenure for women and inverse seniority-based layoff rules, along with part-time status, may account for women's high incidence of displacement. But explaining gender differences in the incidence and consequences of import-competing job loss is a subject for another study. What is clear here is that the burden of import-competing job loss falls on women, in large part because women traditionally have been employed in these high import-competing industries.

Lower educational attainment also describes these lower-wage industries. High school dropouts make up 25 to 50 percent of the displaced from these industries. A few, unbalanced importer industries stand out: textiles, apparel, leather products, and footwear. The fraction of high school dropouts is notably lower in the higher-wage industries, at 7-10 percent. These industries are also either balanced or unbalanced exporters. This point should be clear. We expect our traditional import-competing industries to be relatively low skill, and their displaced workers face readjustment starting from modest levels of formal schooling. Their on-the-job skills are more difficult to observe, but formal schooling and on-the-job training are known to be positively correlated. We should expect these workers to face difficult readjustments (see Field and Graham 1997).

Many high import-competing displaced workers were established in their jobs. Long tenures clearly characterize the high-wage industries. Half of the displaced from tires and inner tubes reported being on the job 10 years or more before their job loss. Even in the low-wage industries, sizable shares (about 20 percent) of displaced workers had been on the job at least 10 years. Just being on a job for 10 years can mean rusty job search skills and a general lack of information about current labor market conditions.

For workers with little formal schooling and long tenure, job loss can be a costly experience. For the high import-competing group as a whole,

Table 3.4 Characteristics of high import-competing industry workers, rank ordered by number of workers displaced, 1979-99

High import-competing industry	Mean old job earnings	Share female	Share high school Dropouts	Graduates	Share with tenure > 10 years	Share reemployed	Change in weekly earnings Median	Mean	Share with earnings loss > 30 percent	Share with joblessness > 26 weeks
Electrical machinery	$412.16	0.484	0.139	0.414	0.184	0.673	−0.033	−0.143	0.22	0.222
Apparel	$236.37	0.791	0.378	0.447	0.181	0.556	−0.041	−0.083	0.199	0.203
Motor vehicles	$448.32	0.248	0.196	0.503	0.287	0.622	−0.117	−0.228	0.35	0.296
Electronic computing equipment	$588.10	0.377	0.068	0.256	0.224	0.737	−0.068	−0.239	0.254	0.134
Radio and television	$431.61	0.479	0.138	0.431	0.214	0.657	−0.003	−0.071	0.192	0.252
Blast furnaces	$509.54	0.111	0.203	0.465	0.39	0.617	−0.36	−0.493	0.446	0.367
Construction and material moving machinery	$489.36	0.178	0.152	0.415	0.219	0.678	−0.17	−0.296	0.307	0.3
Miscellaneous manufacturing industries	$327.01	0.46	0.236	0.416	0.14	0.638	−0.023	−0.173	0.229	0.201
Footwear	$240.26	0.662	0.427	0.439	0.194	0.543	−0.071	−0.072	0.239	0.329
Scientific and controlling instruments	$464.28	0.403	0.087	0.311	0.128	0.717	0.021	−0.088	0.17	0.198
Toys and sporting goods	$333.96	0.506	0.212	0.312	0.117	0.619	−0.03	−0.153	0.245	0.23
Knitting mills	$223.05	0.759	0.368	0.487	0.167	0.609	−0.024	−0.107	0.225	0.263

Other primary metals	$444.22	0.252	0.189	0.563	0.257	0.581	−0.061	−0.157	0.306	0.207
Other rubber products	$311.23	0.533	0.261	0.522	0.297	0.683	0	−0.166	0.231	0.101
Tires and inner tubes	$605.57	0.247	0.085	0.309	0.485	0.689	−0.42	−0.464	0.487	0.315
Photographic equipment	$526.49	0.223	0.137	0.414	0.385	0.777	−0.077	−0.15	0.254	0.236
Cycles and miscellaneous transport	$352.04	0.219	0.221	0.647	0.136	0.681	0	−0.203	0.255	0.251
Leather products	$226.64	0.734	0.525	0.321	0.17	0.378	−0.089	−0.106	0.254	0.335
Office and accounting machines	$464.81	0.432	0.095	0.462	0.167	0.612	0.206	0.175	0.117	0.237
Pottery and related	$267.02	0.454	0.376	0.386	0.229	0.396	−0.223	−0.464	0.338	0.214
Miscellaneous textiles	$282.40	0.666	0.379	0.559	0.222	0.511	−0.077	−0.328	0.398	0.242
Watches, clocks	$403.63	0.268	0.098	0.434	0.241	0.777	0.01	−0.066	0.128	0.169
Leather tanning and finishing	$322.83	0.368	0.098	0.471	0.202	0.635	0.158	0.101	0.092	0.109
High-import-competing average	$402.97	0.449	0.213	0.427	0.221	0.635	−0.047	−0.132	0.253	0.24
Manufacturing average	$396.88	0.369	0.211	0.437	0.215	0.648	−0.047	−0.121	0.252	0.221
Nonmanufacturing average	$368.65	0.511	0.119	0.365	0.127	0.691	0	−0.038	0.212	0.127

Note: Changes in weekly earnings are changes in ln(earnings). See appendix tables D.3 and D.4 for medium and low import-competing industries.

Source: Author's calculations from the Displaced Worker Surveys, 1984-2000, using CPS sampling weights.

the likelihood of reemployment is less than two-thirds (at 63.5 percent), and it varies from a low of 38 percent for leather products to a high of 83 percent for photographic equipment. Almost all of these workers (97 percent) were employed full-time before displacement, making weak labor force attachment, from the worker side, an unlikely cause for the low reemployment rates.

For most high-import-competing workers, the time needed to find a new job is within the usual 26-week period of eligibility for unemployment compensation. Half of these workers had unemployment spells of 8 weeks or less. Interestingly, 27 percent of workers were unemployed for less than 1 week (this group is included in the half with spells of less than 8 weeks). Yet a full quarter of workers were unemployed for more than 26 weeks (6 months), at which point standard unemployment compensation is exhausted. There is a wide variation in the incidence of long spells of unemployment (jobless for 6 months or longer) across the high import-competing industries. In some industries, relatively few workers were jobless 6 months or more (10 percent in other rubber products and leather tanning and finishing), and in others long periods of joblessness were a more likely experience (36.7 percent in blast furnaces, 32.9 percent in footwear, and 31.5 percent in tires and inner tubes).

What about earnings losses? The mean earnings loss was 13.2 percent. The range of earnings losses is striking across the high import-competing industries. Mean earnings losses from two of the high-wage industries were greater than 45 percent (blast furnaces, and tires and inner tubes). Mean earnings losses from other high-wage industries were notably smaller (e.g., motor vehicles at 23 percent and photographic equipment at 15 percent). Low-wage industries have lower mean and median earnings losses, and we expect some of that effect statistically (i.e., high-wage workers have more earnings to "lose" as they drop down in the earnings distribution than do low-wage ones). High-wage industries have a greater share of their workers reporting large (higher than 30 percent) earnings losses. With their predominance in low-wage industries, women have slightly smaller mean earnings losses than men (12 percent compared with 15 percent), a difference that is not statistically significant.

Similar details for the medium and low import-competing industries are reported in appendix tables D.3 and D.4. Differences between our high-import group and these two groups are more subtle than striking. In the rest of manufacturing, women have larger mean earnings losses than men. This result is the reverse of that found for the high import-competing displaced group. Overall, long tenure and modest levels of formal schooling characterize many displaced manufacturing workers.

Summary, and a Look Ahead

This chapter reveals a few points for summary, and points that also look ahead. The characteristics of displacement have changed since the 1980s (see Farber 1997, 2001; Kletzer 1998b). Displaced workers were older, more educated, and more white collar in the 1990s than they were in the 1980s. To little surprise, these characteristics also increasingly describe the workforce (US Department of Labor 1994, 1995). The high import-competing displaced workers examined here are disproportionately blue collar, goods-producing ones; that is, "old-style" displaced workers. At the outset, this means that they may carry into their job loss characteristics that are not in step with growing segments of the economy.

A difficult question is predicting who will find job loss particularly costly. It is difficult to discern clear patterns in the data. Higher predisplacement earnings are associated with larger earnings losses. To learn more, we need to turn to a more detailed examination of the correlates of postdisplacement labor market outcomes. To focus our thoughts, it is useful to remember one of the reasons why job displacement is an important policy question: Displacement involves a combination of losing an established job *and* the need to seek reemployment. This creates the possibility of losses of job- or firm-specific human capital (including job networks), and the risk of permanently lower wages for workers. We will consider factors influencing reemployment first, and then earnings losses.

4

Reemployment after Job Loss

One important observation in chapter 3 was the lower reemployment likelihood for high import-competing displaced workers relative to other displaced manufacturing workers. The key question for this chapter is, what characteristics of workers and industries can explain the gap? I provide answers to these questions by estimating a statistical model of the likelihood of reemployment. In this model, a worker's survey date status is classified as either reemployed or not reemployed.[1] With two exclusive and exhaustive classifications—employed or not employed—the appropriate econometric approach is called binary choice, which is statistically implemented here in a logit (or logistic) estimation.[2] The first set of estimates is reported in table 4.1. The table reports estimates of the change in the probability of reemployment that is associated with a unit change in each explanatory variable. These estimates are of interest because they represent how the likelihood of reemployment changes as an explanatory variable changes. The (direct) coefficient estimates from the logit estimation are reported in appendix table D.5.[3]

---

1. The status "not reemployed" includes unemployment, retirement, going to school, and staying at home. I do not distinguish between these nonemployment states.

2. The logit model is the most common econometric specification for estimating relationships where the dependent variable is qualitative in nature and must be represented as a "0/1" choice—in this case, reemployed (1) or not reemployed (0).

3. These reported estimates are called "marginal effects," and for each explanatory variable they are calculated at the means of the other explanatory variables. An estimated coefficient from a logit specification does not directly produce an estimate of the change in the probability (of reemployment) due to a unit change in the relevant explanatory variable. This probability change is given by the derivative of the probability in the logit model, which is $\beta P(1 - P)$, where P is the sample reemployment rate and β is the coefficient estimate.

Table 4.1 Change in the probability of reemployment, full sample (marginal effects, calculated from logit coefficients)

Characteristic	(1)	(2)	(3)
Manufacturing (nondurable goods)	−0.0598**	−0.0274*	−0.0269**
	(0.0193)	(0.0128)	(0.0104)
Manufacturing (durable goods)	−0.0289*	−0.0226*	−0.0423**
	(0.0129)	(0.0099)	(0.0094)
Transportation, communications,	−0.0098	−0.0027	−0.0259
utilities	(0.0177)	(0.0146)	(0.0142)
Age at displacement (years)			
20-24		0.0940**	0.0851**
		(0.0107)	(0.0110)
25-34		0.1097**	0.1052**
		(0.0079)	(0.0079)
35-44		0.1106**	0.1101**
		(0.0096)	(0.0098)
Education			
High school graduate		0.1058**	0.1116**
		(0.0079)	(0.0081)
Some college		0.1599**	0.1622**
		(0.0083)**	(0.0084)**
College degree or higher		0.2494**	0.2434**
		(0.0093)**	(0.0093)**
Job tenure (years)			
Less than 3		0.0106	0.0191
		(0.0103)	(0.0106)
3-5		0.0376**	0.0463**
		(0.0101)	(0.0104)
6-10		0.0294**	0.0366**
		(0.0104)	(0.0106)
Displaced from full-time job		0.1019**	0.0780**
		(0.0094)	(0.0090)
Minority		−0.1063**	−0.1029**
		(0.0084)	(0.0084)
Married		0.0193**	0.0116
		(0.0070)	(0.0067)
Female			−0.0973**
			(0.0062)
Year displaced			
1979-80	−0.0764**	−0.0747**	−0.0736**
	(0.0150)	(0.0157)	(0.0152)
1984-89	0.0569**	0.0538**	0.0567**
	(0.0086)	(0.0083)	(0.0083)
1990-92	0.0510**	0.0366**	0.0383**
	(0.0088)	(0.0091)	(0.0090)
1993-99	0.1774**	0.1717**	0.1773**
	(0.0098)	(0.0098)	(0.0099)
Years since displacement	0.0828**	0.0794**	0.0805**
	(0.0034)	(0.0037)	(0.0037)
Constant	−0.0911**	−0.3918**	−0.3251**
	(0.0133)	(0.0206)	(0.0212)
Observations	35,435	35,222	35,222

*significant at 5 percent; ** significant at 1 percent.

Note: Standard errors in parentheses.

Source: Author's calculations from the Displaced Worker Surveys, 1984-2000.

The Full Sample

We first use the broad sample of all displaced workers. The full sample (see table 4.1) provides a good opportunity to pin down the influence of certain demographic and labor market characteristics because it offers considerable variation in these characteristics. For the group as a whole, the sample average reemployment rate is 68.1 percent. This means that the "representative" worker in our sample—a displaced worker who is 38 years' old, has 5.3 years' job tenure, has 12.8 years of education, is male, is married, is not a member of a minority group, and who lost a full-time job in wholesale and retail trade, and services in 1989—has a reemployment likelihood of 68 percent.

Turning first to the difference between manufacturing workers and other workers, we find that manufacturing workers are less likely to be reemployed than workers displaced from wholesale and retail trade and services. Column (1) of table 4.1 presents estimates from a very sparse specification, one that controls broadly for industrial sector (of displacement), year of displacement (to account for business cycle effects), and years since displacement (to account for the fact that finding a new job takes time). No individual worker characteristics are included. This pared-down specification asks whether manufacturing workers are less likely to be reemployed than workers displaced from wholesale and retail trade and services in the same year and with the same amount of time since the job loss. We find that nondurable-goods manufacturing workers are 5.9 percentage points less likely to be reemployed, and durable-goods workers are 2.9 percentage points less likely to be reemployed than the similar representative worker displaced from wholesale and retail trade and services. This means that our representative worker, if displaced from nondurable-goods manufacturing, faces a 62 percent likelihood of reemployment; and if displaced from durable-goods manufacturing, a 65.2 percent likelihood of reemployment—relative to the 68 percent likelihood for the wholesale and retail trade and services worker. These differences are statistically significant.

The difference between manufacturing and wholesale and retail trade and services narrows considerably when other factors are included in the specification. In column (2) of table 4.1, when controls for age at displacement, job tenure, educational attainment, racial and ethnic minority status, and full-time status before displacement are added to the set reported on in column (1), both nondurable-goods and durable-goods workers are about 2-3 percentage points less likely to be reemployed than those displaced from wholesale and retail trade and services. This reduces the nondurable-goods effect by about half, and slightly reduces the durable-goods effect. The differences remain statistically significant, though considerably smaller (in the case of nondurable-goods workers). The narrowing of what we will call the "industry effect" is important; it means that individual demographic and labor market characteristics are systematically related to reemployment. If these factors are "doing the work" (i.e., truly explaining differences in reemployment), then policymakers, when looking for potential signals of labor market adjustment difficulties, should turn first to these worker characteristics.

In that spirit, we will consider each characteristic. Age stood out as a clear difference in tables 3.1-3.3. Here, we see that increasing age is strongly negatively related to reemployment. Workers 25-34 or 35-44 years old are about 11 percentage points more likely to be reemployed than workers 45 years old or older at the time of displacement (the reference group).[4] The young and prime-aged (25-44 years old) are much more likely to be reemployed, controlling for these other factors.

Differences by educational attainment are even more striking. In comparison with the reference group of high school dropouts, workers with a college degree (or higher) are 25 percentage points more likely to be reemployed, high school graduates 9.4 percentage points more likely, and workers with some college experience 11 percentage points more likely.

Advanced job tenure is associated with a considerably lower likelihood of reemployment. In comparison with workers with more than 10 years' job tenure, workers with 3-5 years' tenure are about 4 percentage points more likely to be reemployed, and workers with 6-10 years, 2.9 percentage points.

Workers displaced from full-time jobs are about 10 percentage points more likely to be reemployed than otherwise similar workers displaced from part-time jobs. This is consistent with a stronger attachment to the labor market, before the job loss. Married workers are slightly more likely to be reemployed than single ones, at a difference of 1.9 percentage points.

The model also controls for overall business cycle effects through the inclusion of a group of indicator variables for year of displacement.[5] The overall health of the economy and the labor market matters a great deal. These effects can be best seen by predicting the likelihood of reemployment for workers with a given set of characteristics at varying times. For example, a worker displaced from nondurable-goods manufacturing in the strong economy of the mid- to late 1990s (1993-99) who is 45 years of age or older, is a high school dropout, has more than 10 years' tenure on the old job, worked full-time at the time of displacement, is a nonminority, and is married had a predicted probability of reemployment of 53.7

---

4. Each category of explanatory variables (age, education, job tenure) has a reference group that is omitted from the estimation. The logit coefficients (and the reinterpretations as probabilities) are estimates of the difference between the included characteristic and its corresponding (excluded) reference group.

5. Year of displacement effects are grouped into 1979-80, 1981-83, 1984-89, 1990-92, and 1993-99 (with 1981-83 the excluded category). The marginal effects are reported at the bottom of table 4.1.

percent. The same worker, if displaced during the deep 1980s recession (1981-83), had a predicted probability of reemployment of 34.5 percent, about 36 percent lower. Although it may not be enough (particularly for older, less educated, long-tenured workers), a strong labor market clearly provides the necessary setting for displaced workers to find the next job.

We can illustrate other effects. For example, making our nondurable-goods displaced worker younger, say 25-44 years old instead of 45 or older, changes the predicted reemployment likelihood to 65.8 percent from 53.7 percent, a 22 percent increase. Educating our nondurable-goods displaced worker up to a high school diploma from high school dropout has about the same effect: a predicted reemployment likelihood of 65.4 percent. If our 45-year-old worker was a college graduate, the likelihood of reemployment jumps to 78.5 percent. These differences are a striking illustration of the importance of education (which is changeable) and age (which is not) in getting the next job.[6]

Job tenure also is important, although with smaller effects. For our nondurable-goods worker, if a high school dropout and 45 years old, the effect of having 6-10 years' job tenure, instead of more than 10 years, is to raise the reemployment likelihood to 57.1 percent from 53.7 percent. Having 3-5 years' tenure produces a reemployment likelihood of 58 percent. The tenure effects are notable and statistically significant, but are clearly smaller than the effects of education and age. Again, we consider this characteristic not because it is changeable, but as a readily observed predictor of labor market adjustment difficulty.

These results are fully consistent with other studies of job loss.[7] Older workers with low levels of formal schooling and who are established in their jobs (as measured by job tenure) face difficult labor market adjustments. Through work experience, they have gained firm- and industry-specific skills. Adding in low levels of formal schooling, the combination may yield few marketable (or transferable) skills. Considerable job tenure is an indicator that job search skills may be rusty. Age lowers the return on investment in new skills. These straightforward results tell us whom we can expect, statistically, to face labor market adjustment difficulties, although not everyone with these characteristics will do so.

But other characteristics also matter. At the sample mean, minority workers face reemployment rates almost 11 percentage points lower than white workers, and women are almost 10 percentage points less likely to be reemployed (see column 3 of table 4.1). For less-skilled manufacturing workers,

---

6. As this report was being written, "dot-com" layoffs were dominating the business press. The predicted probability of reemployment for a typical "dot-comer"—that is, a worker displaced from the services sector, 25-34 years old, college graduate, less than 3 years' job tenure, full-time, nonminority, and married—was 87.8 percent.

7. See Fallick (1996) and Kletzer (1998b) for reviews.

reemployment differences by race and sex are even larger. To illustrate, if our nondurable-goods worker is a high school dropout, 45 years old or older, has more than 10 years' job tenure, worked full time, is a nonminority, was displaced in 1993-99, and is female, her predicted reemployment likelihood is 47.5 percent. If this worker is male, however, his reemployment likelihood increases to 58.6 percent, a 23.3 percent (or 11.1 percentage point) increase. If the female worker is a racial or ethnic minority,[8] her reemployment likelihood falls by 24 percent, to 36 percent. If the male worker belongs to a racial or ethnic minority group, his reemployment likelihood is 46.8 percent, 20 percent lower.

Although the effect of being female is large, it is important, for reasons detailed below, to point out that the sum of the other effects (e.g., age, education, and job tenure) greatly reduces the estimate of the industry effect, whereas the addition of a control for gender only incrementally reduces the industry effect. This can be seen in table 4.1 by comparing the size of the estimates in column (2), without the control for gender, to the estimates in column (3), with the gender control. Most of the reduction in the industry effect occurs from columns (1) to (2), with the addition of the controls other than gender.

With all the controls, a nondurable-goods displaced worker faces a reemployment rate that is 2.7 percentage points lower, and a durable-goods one a reemployment rate 4.2 percentage points lower, as compared with otherwise similar workers displaced from wholesale and retail trade and services. Without any other factors, a nondurable-goods job loss has a reemployment rate 5.9 percentage points lower and a durable-goods one 2.9 percentage points lower. The nondurable-goods industry effect persists, but it is smaller by half after accounting for age, education, job tenure, minority status, and gender. The durable-goods industry effect is actually larger after accounting for these important worker characteristics. This means that durable-goods industries have fewer women, racial and ethnic minorities, older workers, and less educated workers than nondurable-goods industries and that, in part, these differences account for their higher reemployment rates relative to nondurable-goods ones.

To summarize, manufacturing workers are less likely to be reemployed than otherwise similar workers displaced from wholesale and retail trade and services. The difference is larger for durable-goods workers than for nondurable-goods workers.[9]

---

8. Defined here, from the CPS, as black, Hispanic, Asian/Pacific Islander, or American Indian.

9. Some other factors, related to industry, such as local labor market conditions and industry growth rates, may be important, but are not included in the specification due to measurement issues.

The Manufacturing Sample

When we turn to high import-competing displaced workers, we limit the sample to manufacturing. The same technique, logit estimation, was applied to this smaller sample, with results reported in table 4.2 for the marginal effects and appendix table D.6 for the estimated logit coefficients. For manufacturing workers, the sample reemployment rate was 64.7 percent. The first step separates workers into the three levels of import competition (high, medium, and low), without any other controls. Estimates from this simple starting point are reported in column (1). Workers from our high-import group were 4.1 percentage points less likely to be reemployed than workers displaced from the low-import group, a statistically significant difference, with no significant difference between the medium and low groups. This is fully consistent with the descriptive differences discussed in chapter 3.

The addition of worker characteristics has both similar and different effects from the full sample discussed above. The addition in column (2) of table 4.2 of age, education, job tenure, full-time status, and minority and marital status reduces the high-import effect, but not by much. High-import workers, controlling for these important characteristics, are still a statistically significant 3.4 percentage points less likely to be reemployed than low-import workers. The effects of these worker characteristics are very similar to the full sample. Prime-aged workers (25-44 years old) have reemployment rates 11 percentage points higher than workers above the age of 45; workers with some college or a college degree experience higher reemployment rates of 14-27 percentage points; and minority workers are 11 percentage points less likely to be reemployed.

To illustrate the large impact of business cycle conditions, we can use the same predictive techniques as was done above for the full sample. A worker displaced from a full-time job in a high import-competing industry in 1981-83, if age 45 years or older, a high school dropout, with more than 10 years' tenure, a nonminority, and married, had a reemployment likelihood of 30.4 percent. The same worker, displaced during the strong(er) labor market of 1993-99, faced a reemployment likelihood of 49.7 percent, an improvement of 19 percentage points, or 63 percent. As a group, manufacturing workers are markedly hampered in their reemployment efforts by a weak economy and labor market.

If our high import-competing worker is younger, between 35 and 44 years of age, and was displaced during the mid- to late 1990s, the reemployment likelihood increases to 61.8 percent from 49.7 percent. Somewhat similarly, if our age 45 years or older worker completed high school instead of dropping out, the reemployment likelihood increases to 61.2 percent from 49.7 percent. The effect of more formal schooling is stronger for younger workers than for older ones. For example, if our younger (age 35-44) worker had a high school diploma, the reemployment likeli-

Table 4.2 Change in the probability of reemployment, manufacturing sample (marginal effects, calculated from logit coefficients)

Characteristic	(1)	(2)	(3)	(4)
High import-competing	-0.0408*	-0.0345**	-0.0206	-0.0206
	(0.0198)	(0.0124)	(0.0130)	(0.0134)
Medium import-competing	-0.0068	0.0002	-0.0030	-0.0040
	(0.0160)	(0.0141)	(0.0126)	(0.0126)
Age at displacement (years)				
20-24		0.1074**	0.0944**	0.1065**
		(0.0209)	(0.0206)	(0.0208)
25-34		0.1196**	0.1122**	0.1185**
		(0.0137)	(0.0138)	(0.0136)
35-44		0.1115**	0.1090**	0.1126**
		(0.0180)	(0.0186)	(0.0186)
Education				
High school graduate		0.1050**	0.1063**	0.1090**
		(0.0118)	(0.0119)	(0.0121)
Some college		0.1456**	0.1392**	0.1387**
		(0.0126)	(0.0128)	(0.0132)
College degree or higher		0.2716**	0.2554**	0.2540**
		(0.0167)	(0.0177)	(0.0178)
Job tenure (years)				
Less than 3		0.0422**	0.0576**	0.0619**
		(0.0135)	(0.0141)	(0.0143)
3-5		0.0644**	0.0788**	0.0836**
		(0.0150)	(0.0156)	(0.0159)
6-10		0.0652**	0.0758**	0.0798**
		(0.0141)	(0.0140)	(0.0142)
Displaced from full-time job		0.1117**	0.0818**	0.0722*
		(0.0297)	(0.0305)	(0.0301)
Minority		-0.1111**	-0.1024**	-0.1056**
		(0.0138)	(0.0141)	(0.0142)
Married		0.0388**	0.0284**	0.1068
		(0.0098)	(0.0097)	(0.0140)
Female			-0.1049**	0.0023
			(0.0111)	(0.0136)
Female × married				-0.1768**
				(0.0260)
Year displaced				
1979-80	-0.0968**	-0.0979**	-0.0949**	
	(0.0212)	(0.0236)	(0.0228)	
1984-89	0.0684**	0.0726**	0.0744**	
	(0.0123)	(0.0118)	(0.0120)	
1990-92	0.0551**	0.0487**	0.0491**	
	(0.0136)	(0.0140)	(0.0134)	
1993-99	0.1803**	0.1854**	0.1901**	
	(0.0152)	(0.0170)	(0.0174)	
Years since displacement	0.0944**	0.0935**	0.0941**	
	(0.0048)	(0.0055)	(0.0058)	
Constant	-0.1392**	-0.4903**	-0.4263**	-0.4770**
	(0.0191)	(0.0375)	(0.0355)	(0.0357)
Observations	13,846	13,795	13,795	13,795

*significant at 5 percent; ** significant at 1 percent.

Note: Standard errors in parentheses.

Source: Author's calculations from the Displaced Worker Surveys, 1984-2000.

hood would rise to 72.1 percent. This point is very important: It informs us that the value of more schooling (or training), in helping reemployment, depends on a worker's other characteristics and therefore is not the same for all workers.[10]

The influence of job tenure is a bit weaker. Workers with 3-10 years' tenure are about 6 percentage points more likely to be reemployed than ones with more than 10 years' tenure. For our high import-competing worker, age 45 years or older, a high school dropout, lowering job tenure to 6-9 years from more than 10 increases the reemployment likelihood to 56.9 percent from 49.7 percent.

So far, the manufacturing sample yields estimates that are qualitatively similar to those for the full sample. In contrast to the full-sample estimates, however, the industry effect, measured here as "high or medium import," relative to low import-competing, is considerably reduced, and loses statistical significance, with the addition of a control for gender. This can be seen by comparing the first row of columns (2), (3), and (4) of table 4.2. The estimated effects of the variables remain basically the same, and the high-import effect falls by about 40 percent and is statistically indistinguishable from zero. This means that the difference in reemployment between the high import-competing industries and the rest of manufacturing is due almost entirely to the much lower (by 10 percentage points) reemployment rates of females, who are predominantly employed in and displaced from the high import-competing industries.

This strong "female" effect found in manufacturing differs from that found in the full sample of industries, where women are also found less likely to be reemployed. The employment of women by industry is much less concentrated across all industries than it is just within manufacturing, where women are very concentrated in nondurable-goods employment. The concentration of female employment in manufacturing means that any industry effect will be confounded with a "female" effect, making it particularly important to use statistical analysis, if possible, to separate the two effects. The difference in the estimates between columns (2) and (3) shows that it is the lower likelihood of reemployment for women that produces the (slightly) lower reemployment likelihood of high import-competing displaced workers, and not the reverse.

We can advance our thinking about this confounding of effects one more step, through an insight obtained from a number of labor market studies.[11] It is broadly established that the association between certain labor market outcomes and marital status differs between men and

---

10. One of the advantages of the nonlinear logit estimation is its ability to discern differences in the effect of changing any given explanatory variable, depending on the values of the other explanatory variables.

11. See Korenman and Neumark (1991, 1992) for leading examples.

women. For example, being married is very often associated with a wage premium for men and a wage penalty for women. One interpretation is that married men are more productive in the workplace than single men, due to their greater responsibilities, and this is reflected in higher earnings. For women, the marriage penalty is often associated with carrying primary child care responsibilities and thus is more of a child penalty than a marriage penalty per se. Without straying too far from our focus, it can be seen that the effect of being female on reemployment estimated here is actually a married *and* female effect. Column (4) of table 4.2 reports these estimates. For the manufacturing sample, a single woman, with our "representative" characteristics, has a reemployment likelihood (of 45.3 percent) indistinguishable from an otherwise comparable single man (45.1 percent), whereas a married woman's reemployment rate of 37.8 percent is 7.3 percentage points lower than a single man's and 19 percentage points lower than a married man's (56.8 percent). The effect of marriage for men is to raise their likelihood of reemployment by about 11 percentage points.

Why are married women so much less likely to be reemployed? This nationally representative sample does not provide much information for further investigation. One clear possibility is that married women—within dual-earner families where theirs may be the lower-income job—face more constrained job searches after displacement due to the jobs of their spouses. Relocation is likely more difficult and costly. There may also be child care constraints or substitution to nonmarket work when displaced.[12]

Summary

What do we conclude about high import competition and one of the costs of job loss? One clear interpretation of this analysis (and others) is that import competition is associated with low reemployment rates because the workers vulnerable to rising import job loss experience difficulty gaining reemployment on the basis of their individual characteristics. It is not import competition per se; it is who gets displaced from (and is employed by) industries with rising import competition. What limits the reemployment of import-competing displaced workers? The same characteristics that limit the reemployment of all displaced workers: low educational attainment, advancing age, high tenure, minority status, and

---

12. From information in the DWSs, we know that nonreemployed men and women are engaged in different activities. Across the survey years, about 18 percent of nonreemployed women are looking for work, as compared with 45 percent of nonreemployed men. Sixty-three percent of nonreemployed women report themselves out of the labor force and at home, as compared with 3 percent of men. Finally, 32 percent of nonreemployed men report retirement, relative to 9 percent of women. I leave this point for future research.

marital status. Married women, even those displaced from full-time jobs, are much less likely to be reemployed.[13] Whether and how this matters for policy will be discussed in chapter 7.

As we see, losing a job and having to find another can be difficult for many workers. The difficulties, however, may not end with reemployment. If the new job pays less than the old one, the costs of job loss can continue for years. We turn next to the question of reemployment earnings and earnings losses.

---

13. What we do not know is why. In future research, it will be important to try to separate the labor supply and labor demand components of this relationship.

5

Understanding Earnings Losses

The descriptive discussion in chapter 3 reveals a few straightforward facts about earnings losses for displaced workers. For manufacturing workers, reemployment is often at a level of pay well below the pay on the old job. On average, weekly earnings from the new job are 13 percent below those from the old one.[1] There is wide variation around this average. About a third of workers earn as much or more from the new job, and about a quarter realize losses greater than 30 percent. The goal of this chapter is to explain that variation in earnings losses. We will start with some background from studies of wage determination, followed by lessons from earlier studies. From this foundation, we will consider the evidence more directly.

Background: Human Capital and Wage Determination

To explain the reasons for earnings losses is a complex problem that requires drawing on theories of human capital and wage determination. The evidence shows that displaced workers were typically earning more in their previous job than they could have earned from other employers.

---

1. This earnings loss estimate is likely an understatement. It considers old job earnings at their level at the time of job loss. If a worker had remained on the job and experienced earnings growth, then it is this higher level of pay that should be compared with the earnings from the new job. The Displaced Worker Surveys offer no such comparison group of individuals who stay on the old jobs.

The challenge is to isolate which factors are responsible for the earnings premium, and therefore for the earnings losses. Some of the likely candidates for such wage premiums are the development of nontransferable human capital in a job, unionization, good job matches, efficiency wages, internal labor markets, and incentive pay mechanisms. Here I will summarize, briefly, some common understandings of the relationship between skills, job tenure, and earnings. Interested readers are directed to Kletzer (1998b) for a more complete discussion.

Human capital models often divide capital into "general capital," which is widely applicable to many employers, and "specific capital," which can be unique to a certain employer or job. In particular, firm-specific human capital is valued only by the current employer and is not transferable across employers. Workers acquire these specific skills through on-the-job training or in classroom training provided by the employer, and as the stock of these skills rises with tenure with the firm, earnings also rise. If firm-specific skills are an important determinant of earnings, workers displaced from their jobs are likely to experience large and perhaps persistent earnings losses. Of course, the line between specific and general human capital is somewhat porous; specific capital may also be transferable to a limited degree.

Job tenure is often the first observable characteristic under consideration, because tenure is the common measure of firm- and job-specific skills. It is clear that earnings losses rise with previous job tenure. Farber (1997) found that each year of job tenure is associated with an additional earnings loss of 1.0-1.3 percent. Topel (1990) estimated that when a worker with 10 years' tenure is displaced, postdisplacement wages will be 25 percent lower. Although previous job tenure is still valued on the new job, its value is less on that job than it was on the old one. For example, before displacement, a blue collar worker with the average amount of predisplacement tenure (5.9 years) earned about 20 percent more than a similar worker with no tenure. Postdisplacement, the worker with 5.9 years predisplacement tenure earned 6.4 percent more than the one with no tenure. This is consistent with a reduction in the value of (old-job) specific skills. For a male white collar worker with average tenure of 6.1 years on the job lost, the predisplacement earnings difference over a similar worker with no tenure was 22.5 percent, and the postdisplacement earnings difference was 19.1 percent (see Kletzer 1989). The far larger dropoff in the contribution of predisplacement tenure to postdisplacement earnings for blue collar workers reveals the importance of factors such as specific human capital and the returns to seniority in production (unionized) jobs for these workers. In contrast, individual ability and transferable skills are a more important part of the returns to tenure for the white collar group.

One important finding is that full- or part-time status before and after displacement plays an important role in determining earnings changes.

Workers reemployed in part-time jobs have significantly larger earnings losses than workers reemployed full-time. Farber (1997) reports that across the surveys, just 12 percent of displaced workers lost part-time jobs, whereas 17 percent of those reemployed at the survey date were in part-time jobs. This suggests a movement from full- to part-time employment. Kletzer (1998a) estimates that workers displaced from full-time jobs and reemployed part-time experience earnings losses 40 percent larger than workers reemployed full-time. Although some of this observed survey-date part-time status may be due to individual labor supply decisions, it seems likely that an inability to find full-time work characterizes many displacement experiences.

Because the Displaced Worker Surveys do not provide information on hourly wages, it is impossible to sort out the extent to which changes in earnings are due to changes in hourly pay or to changes in hours worked. As one approach to this question, researchers have focused on the subsample of workers displaced from and reemployed in full-time jobs. Although earnings losses are smaller on average for this group than for displaced workers as a whole, they are still a sizable 9 percent over time (Farber 1997).

This point about full- and part-time work is more broadly indicative of a limitation of the Displaced Worker Surveys in the study of earnings changes. Individual characteristics easily measured in these surveys, such as education and job tenure, change very little before and after job loss and therefore cannot explain much of the earnings difference. We do know that earnings losses are smaller for more educated workers and larger for more tenured workers. But in general only a small fraction of the variation in earnings changes across workers is explained by the traditional explanatory variables.

The key factors that do change (or that can potentially change) are hours worked, industry, and occupation. It has been shown, in many studies, that earnings losses are larger for workers who change industry or occupation or who work fewer hours (see Kletzer 1998b). There is, however, a circularity to using changes in these factors to explain earnings losses, because changes in these characteristics of work are an outcome of job loss on equal footing with earnings changes. In other words, it should not be surprising that characteristics of the new job, as compared with the old job, help account for earnings change. Statistically, the addition of these changes to our estimation models should enhance the explanatory power of our earnings change estimates. Yet these very characteristics are what we seek to understand, as outcomes, and therefore they are problematic when included as explanatory variables.

Looking More Closely at Changes in Earnings

With these data limitations in mind, table 5.1 reports a straightforward (ordinary least squares) regression analysis of the change in weekly earn-

Table 5.1 Change in weekly earnings for workers reemployed at their survey date, full sample (ordinary least squares estimates)

Characteristic	(1)	(2)	(3)
Manufacturing (nondurable goods)	−0.0492**	−0.0201	−0.0196
	(0.0115)	(0.0115)	(0.0115)
Manufacturing (durable goods)	−0.0846**	−0.0623**	−0.0632**
	(0.0094)	(0.0096)	(0.0096)
Transportation, communications,	−0.1042**	−0.0895**	−0.0907**
utilities	(0.0143)	(0.0142)	(0.0142)
Age at displacement (years)			
20-24		0.1421**	0.1464**
		(0.0135)	(0.0135)
25-34		0.1021**	0.1045**
		(0.0107)	(0.0107)
35-44		0.0608**	0.0628**
		(0.0109)	(0.0109)
Education			
High school graduate		0.0261*	0.0274*
		(0.0124)	(0.0124)
Some college		0.0202	0.0201
		(0.0132)	(0.0132)
College degree or higher		0.0636**	0.0639**
		(0.0138)	(0.0138)
Job tenure (years)			
Less than 3		0.1829**	0.1849**
		(0.0122)	(0.0122)
3-5		0.1037**	0.1057**
		(0.0129)	(0.0129)
6-10		0.0610**	0.0623**
		(0.0141)	(0.0141)
Minority		0.0035	0.0031
		(0.0113)	(0.0113)
Married		0.0137	0.0490**
		(0.0079)	(0.0108)
Female		−0.0254**	0.0184
		(0.0079)	(0.0120)
Female × married			−0.0752**
			(0.0155)
Years since displacement	0.0021	0.0077*	0.0076*
	(0.0034)	(0.0034)	(0.0034)
Constant	0.4633**	0.1781**	0.1526**
	(0.0179)	(0.0250)	(0.0255)
Observations	18,565	18,565	18,565
Adjusted R^2	0.10	0.13	0.13

*significant at 5 percent; ** significant at 1 percent.

Note: Dependent variable is change in ln(earnings). Year of displacement and full-time status (at displacement) included as controls. Standard errors in parentheses.

ings, for the full sample of workers reemployed at their survey date. Without controls for worker characteristics, there are sizable differences by sector in earnings losses. As we saw more descriptively above, manufacturing workers (and transportation and public utilities workers) experience larger earnings losses than displaced workers in wholesale and retail trade and services. Transportation and utilities workers experience earnings losses about 11 percent larger than workers in wholesale and retail trade and services, and durable-goods manufacturing workers' earnings losses are about 8.8 percent larger. Nondurable-goods workers, and the low-wage sector overall, experience earnings losses 5 percent larger than workers in wholesale and retail trade and services.

The addition of controls for age at displacement, educational attainment, job tenure, gender, minority status, marital status, and full-time status reduces the sectoral (or industry) effect. Nondurable-goods workers do not experience larger earnings losses once these demographic and human-capital characteristics are included. The larger earnings losses of (high-wage) durable-goods and transportation and public utilities workers remain, reduced in size to a 6.4-9.4 percent larger loss than similar workers displaced from wholesale and retail trade and services.

Adding to our emerging profile of workers who experience costly job losses, earnings losses rise with previous job tenure and age and are smaller for more educated workers. All else remaining the same, earnings losses are 21 percent smaller for workers with less than 3 years' tenure, relative to workers with more than 10 years' tenure. For workers with 3-5 years' tenure, earnings losses are 11 percent smaller. Prime-aged workers, those 25-44 years old, have earnings losses 6-11 percent smaller than workers older than 45. Earnings losses are somewhat larger (2.6 percent) for women. The estimated difference between minority and nonminority workers is small and statistically insignificant. Column (3) of table 5.1 separates the effects of marriage and gender. Marriage narrows earnings losses for men and increases earnings losses for women. There is no statistically significant penalty for single women.

Among manufacturing workers (table 5.2), earnings changes are not significantly related to the degree of import competition. Even without any of the worker controls, high import-competing workers do not have significantly larger earnings losses than the less import-competing group. Worker characteristics matter similarly to the discussion above: Earnings losses increase with tenure on the old job and age at displacement. Losses are smaller for more educated workers. Within manufacturing, earnings-loss differences between men and women are not statistically significant.

With the Displaced Worker Surveys, we obtain a short-run, or snapshot, view of earnings losses because the time horizon is about 1-3 years after job loss. These sizable short-run earnings losses prompt a natural next question about long-run earnings opportunities and losses. The Displaced

Table 5.2 Change in weekly earnings for workers reemployed at their survey date, manufacturing sample (ordinary least squares estimates)

Characteristic	(1)	(2)	(3)
High import-competing	−0.0199	−0.0058	−0.0058
	(0.0163)	(0.0161)	(0.0161)
Medium import-competing	−0.0187	−0.0097	−0.0101
	(0.0160)	(0.0157)	(0.0157)
Age at displacement (years)			
20-24		0.1127**	0.1152**
		(0.0208)	(0.0208)
25-34		0.0891**	0.0902**
		(0.0161)	(0.0162)
35-44		0.0530**	0.0540**
		(0.0162)	(0.0162)
Education			
High school graduate		0.0051	0.0056
		(0.0160)	(0.0160)
Some college		0.0047	0.0046
		(0.0183)	(0.0183)
College degree or higher		0.0537**	0.0533**
		(0.0198)	(0.0198)
Job tenure (years)			
Less than 3		0.2174**	0.2184**
		(0.0174)	(0.0174)
3-5		0.1302**	0.1311**
		(0.0181)	(0.0181)
6-10		0.0909**	0.0918**
		(0.0194)	(0.0194)
Minority		−0.0006	−0.0007
		(0.0169)	(0.0169)
Married		0.0315*	0.0471**
		(0.0123)	(0.0156)
Female		−0.0184	0.0060
		(0.0123)	(0.0194)
Female × married			−0.0400
			(0.0247)
Years since displacement	−0.0051	0.0036	0.0035
	(0.0050)	(0.0050)	(0.0050)
Constant	0.3424**	0.0359	0.0241
	(0.0371)	(0.0434)	(0.0440)
Observations	7,167	7,167	7,167
Adjusted R^2	0.03	0.07	0.07

*significant at 5 percent; **significant at 1 percent.

Note: Dependent variable is change in ln(earnings). Year of displacement and full-time status (at displacement) included as controls. Standard errors in parentheses.

Worker Surveys cannot be used to answer long-run earnings questions, but a handful of earlier studies used data that follow a set of workers over time. In summary, earnings losses are large and persistent, on the order of 25 percent, 5-10 years after job loss. (Readers interested in more detail about these studies are directed to appendix C.)

The Importance of Industry for Earnings Change

Import-competing job loss, by its nature, is concentrated in a set of industries. A small number of displaced-worker studies show that "industry" matters, by revealing that industry (or more broadly sector) may be an important dimension across which skills are transferable. These studies find that the postdisplacement earnings of individuals who change industry are lower than the earnings of otherwise comparable individuals who stay in the same industry (see references in Kletzer 1998b). For manufacturing workers, Jacobson, LaLonde, and Sullivan (1993) found larger earning losses for workers reemployed outside manufacturing than for workers who remained in manufacturing upon reemployment. Larger earnings losses for workers who change industry may not necessarily reflect lost specific human capital. Industry wage effects due to efficiency wages, union rents, incentive pay schemes, or internal labor markets may partially account for the earnings losses.

More broadly, common sense provides a strong push toward thinking that it matters a great deal where a displaced worker becomes reemployed. More detailed economic analysis has been a bit slow to embrace this point, in part because there are few theoretical guidelines to suggest a model of industry (or sectoral) reemployment. The guidance from theory may be scant, but it is there. A foundation of research in wage determination notes that an individual's ability to retain human capital or a share of industry rents (rents due to unionization or incentive pay premiums) or to retain hierarchical standing that was due to promotion-from-within policies (internal labor markets) is very likely to depend on the "new" industry and occupation. Workers who regain employment in the same, or similar, industry and/or occupation are more likely to retain their human capital, as well as other industry effects. Thus, where workers become reemployed is unlikely to be random, and it is likely related to postdisplacement earnings potential.

A small number of studies have estimated models of industry mobility after job displacement. The approach of these studies is usually to characterize industry mobility as reemployment in either the "same" industry or in a "different" industry (generally defined at the 2-digit SIC level). These studies find that mobility between industries depends on wages in the various industries; the job opportunities in different sectors (Kletzer

1992; Fallick 1993; Seitchik and Zornitsky 1989); if the education level of the displaced worker is high enough to allow movement into a broader range of expanding sectors (Fallick 1993); and whether the benefits of job tenure within an existing job or industry are high and transferable within the industry (Neal 1995; Kletzer 1996). In general, these results underscore earlier findings (Topel 1990; Carrington 1993; and Jacobson, LaLonde, and Sullivan 1993) that a substantial share of earnings losses results from the loss of highly firm-specific earnings components. These results imply that industry-specific skills may retain their value if an individual becomes reemployed in a similar sector where those skills are in demand.

Understanding why workers change industry will remain an important question for the research literature on earnings losses. In the following chapter, I consider whether and how import-competing displaced workers change industry after losing their job.

6

Where Are Import-Competing Displaced Workers Reemployed?

This chapter examines the pattern of reemployment by industrial sector. It extends earlier research reported in Kletzer (2000). The focus is on how earnings changes vary by reemployment sector, which will help explain the range of outcomes available to displaced workers.

This discussion is also applicable to a larger question in the literature on trade and wages: In what "directions" does foreign competition reallocate labor across industries? The linkages between changing trade patterns and changing employment patterns have been examined in a number of studies, including Borjas, Freeman, and Katz (1992, 1997), and Sachs and Shatz (1994, 1998). These studies confirm that the rise of net imports from developing countries is low-skill intensive relative to the rest of manufacturing and the economy. One implication of these studies is that job loss in manufacturing will release relatively unskilled workers into the labor market and that reemployment of these workers in the (low-wage) services sector provides one avenue for downward pressure on wages with increasing trade. This possible outcome associates economywide labor reallocation with economywide increasing earnings inequality. My focus here is narrower, and directed to implications for individual workers of reemployment in a sector different from the one where jobs were lost. This focus is most appropriate for explaining the individual costs of import-competing job displacement.

Reemployment Sector and Earnings Changes

Figure 6.1 presents a summary of where high import-competing workers are reemployed, by broad industrial sector, and the mean earnings change

Figure 6.1 Reemployment and mean earnings changes for high import-competing workers, by industrial sector

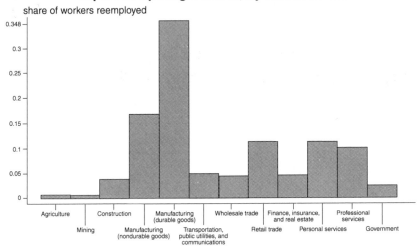

share of workers reemployed

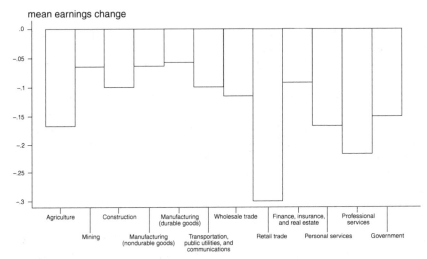

mean earnings change

Notes: The top bar graph reports the share of workers reemployed in each sector; the height of the bar is the fraction or share reemployed. The bottom bar graph reports mean earnings changes; the height of the bar is the percentage change in weekly earnings. More precisely, the earnings change reported in the lower bar graph is the change in log(earnings). To convert to a percentage change in earnings, we multiply the reported number by 100.

Source: Author's calculations from Displaced Worker Surveys, 1984-2000.

for workers reemployed in each sector. Figures 6.2 and 6.3 present the same data for medium and low import-competing workers. Table 6.1 reports the more detailed information from which the figures were drawn.[1]

A few general observations stand out. First, contrary to common perceptions, not all displaced manufacturing workers are reemployed at McDonald's. Overall, just 10 percent of reemployed manufacturing workers are in retail trade (McDonald's, as an eating and drinking establishment, is in the retail trade sector). High import-competing displaced workers are no more likely than any other manufacturing worker to be reemployed in retail trade. In contrast, 21 percent of nonmanufacturing displaced workers are reemployed in retailing.

Second, there is considerable reemployment within manufacturing. High import-competing displaced workers—100 percent of whom were displaced from nondurable- and durable-goods manufacturing—are being reemployed in manufacturing, at a level of about half. Sixteen percent are reemployed in nondurable goods, and 35 percent in durable goods (0.164 + 0.355 = 0.519). That is, considering just those workers reemployed when surveyed (about two-thirds of those displaced), fully half of import-competing displaced workers are reemployed back in manufacturing. This high rate of return among the reemployed is likely contrary to casual expectations. At the same time, fully half of displaced manufacturing workers, upon reemployment, are leaving their old sector. The return rate is also lower when we note that it refers only to the two-thirds reemployed. Incorporating the 0.634 reemployment rate, we note that about a third (0.329) of all high import-competing displaced workers return to manufacturing after losing their job. Another third are reemployed in nonmanufacturing sectors, and the remaining third are not reemployed.

Workers who return to their old sector may retain the value of some specific skills, keep earning union rents, and maintain their position in internal job ladders. All these factors are expected to mitigate earnings losses, and they do, as displayed in the lower bar graph of figure 6.1. For manufacturing workers, regaining employment in manufacturing greatly reduces earnings losses. Mean earnings losses are smallest for workers reemployed in durable goods (at 4.5 percent), and next smallest in nondu-

---

1. The table is a very basic "reemployment matrix," reporting the industrial sector from which workers were displaced (categorized by the level of import-competition of their old industry) and the industrial sector of reemployment. The table contains four main rows, labeled "high," "medium," and "low" (for the import-competing nature of the manufacturing industries) and "nonmanufacturing" for the remaining private nonmanufacturing sectors (utilities, wholesale and retail trade, services). This last row serves as a comparison group for manufacturing. Workers are displaced from one of these four big rows. They are reemployed in one of 12 columns that designate new industrial sectors. Within each cell, defined as a main row intersecting with a column, five measures are reported.

Figure 6.2 Reemployment and mean earnings changes for medium import-competing workers, by industrial sector

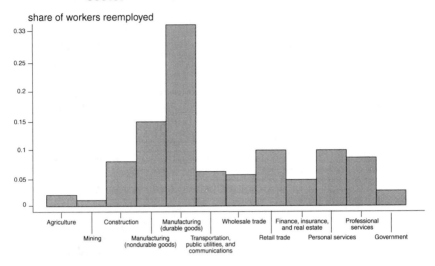

share of workers reemployed

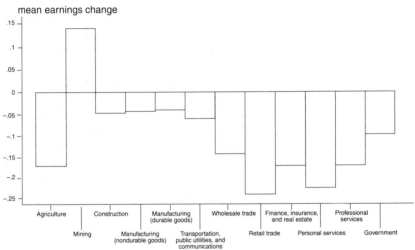

mean earnings change

Source: Author's calculations from Displaced Worker Surveys, 1984-2000.

rable goods (5.8 percent). Median earnings losses are even smaller, at no loss for durable goods and 3.7 percent for nondurable goods.

Although earnings losses are small for the average high import-competing worker reemployed in manufacturing, there is still considerable variation in earnings changes. About a fifth of these workers suffer earnings

Figure 6.3 Reemployment and mean earnings changes for low import-competing workers, by industrial sector

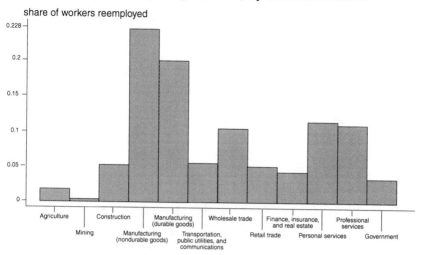

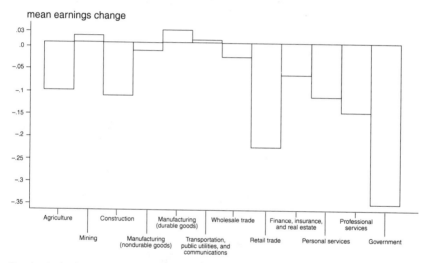

Source: Author's calculations from Displaced Worker Surveys, 1984-2000.

losses in excess of 30 percent (see table 6.1). Even within manufacturing, skilled (but older) workers may find themselves unfamiliar with standards, processes, and procedures instituted by manufacturing firms since the mid-1980s (see Powers and Markusen 1999). That 20 percent of workers with very large earnings losses is, however, considerably smaller than the corresponding shares for workers reemployed in other sectors.

Table 6.1 Reemployment sector, earnings losses, and jobless durations, by industry level of import competition

Level of import competition	Agriculture	Mining	Construction	Manufacturing Nondurables	Durables	TCU	Trade Wholesale	Retail	Finance, insurance, real estate	Services Personal, business	Professional	Government	Total
High													
Number of workers	19,379	23,672	190,065	853,687	1,887,237	259,336	221,516	556,987	214,245	524,750	462,936	93,906	5,307,716
Share	0.0036	0.0044	0.0358	0.1608	0.3555	0.0488	0.0417	0.1049	0.0403	0.0988	0.0883	0.0176	1
Median earnings change	−0.181	−0.078	−0.086	−0.037	0	−0.01	−0.07	−0.262	0	−0.113	−0.149	−0.128	−0.048
Mean earnings change	−0.294	−0.064	−0.13	−0.058	−0.045	−0.118	−0.133	−0.334	−0.058	−0.223	−0.255	−0.062	−0.125
Median weeks jobless	38	9	12	8	6	6	8	8	6	6	13	10	8
Medium													
Number of workers	67,091	27,302	394,009	949,850	2,089,635	302,265	257,804	538,684	217,211	551,787	470,198	131,914	5,997,750
Share	0.0112	0.0045	0.0656	0.1583	0.3484	0.0503	0.0429	0.0898	0.0362	0.0919	0.0783	0.0219	1
Median earnings change	−0.261	−0.041	−0.053	−0.023	−0.029	0	−0.131	−0.251	−0.136	−0.228	−0.197	−0.055	−0.063
Mean earnings change	−0.29	0.144	−0.062	−0.034	−0.041	−0.075	−0.149	−0.29	−0.218	−0.298	−0.225	−0.114	−0.118
Median weeks jobless	6	10	6	4	6	9	6	8	9	6	8	8	6
Low													
Number of workers	31,944	3,943	125,304	559,789	535,946	156,584	125,062	261,557	93,893	281,170	299,028	61,134	2,535,354
Share	0.0125	0.0015	0.0494	0.2207	0.2113	0.0617	0.0493	0.1032	0.037	0.1109	0.1179	0.0241	1
Median earnings change	−0.048	0.182	0	−0.006	0.018	0	−0.043	−0.19	0.018	−0.052	−0.163	−0.331	−0.028
Mean earnings change	−0.157	0.008	−0.155	−0.012	0.026	0.048	−0.052	−0.217	−0.074	−0.15	−0.166	−0.393	−0.077
Median weeks jobless	8	0	8	4	5	6	4	6	4	6	10	7	6
Nonmanufacturing													
Number of workers	164,442	62,076	896,199	951,046	1,491,502	2,172,656	1,324,330	4,488,224	2,276,067	3,368,766	4,659,912	579,645	22,400,000
Share	0.0073	0.0027	0.04	0.0424	0.0665	0.0969	0.0591	0.2003	0.1016	0.1504	0.208	0.0258	1
Median earnings change	−0.062	0.084	0	0.003	0.051	0	0	−0.028	0.001	0	0	0.039	0
Mean earnings change	−0.113	0.086	0.016	0.039	0.073	0.009	0.009	−0.037	−0.019	−0.034	0.007	0.101	−0.003
Median weeks jobless	3	4	4	5	3	3	4	3	4	4	3	6	4

TCU = Transportation, communications, and utilities.

Note: Changes in earnings are changes in ln (earnings).

Source: Author's calculations from the Displaced Worker Surveys, 1984–2000.

Displaced manufacturing workers who gain reemployment in manufacturing also experience the shortest median period of joblessness (6-8 weeks), as compared with workers reemployed elsewhere. This may be a result of searching first in familiar labor markets in manufacturing, and turning to less familiar markets and networks only after a period of unsuccessful searching. These spells of joblessness are well within the standard period of eligibility for unemployment compensation (26 weeks).

Wholesale and retail trade, finance, and services provide about 35 percent of import-competing displaced-worker reemployment. Mean earnings changes are highly variable, ranging from a 6 percent loss in finance, insurance, and real estate to a 34 percent loss in retail trade. A large share of such workers (25-40 percent) report earnings losses exceeding 30 percent. Retail trade and business and personal services together account for nearly 20 percent of import-competing displaced reemployment, and mean earnings losses are large (22-33 percent). Given the prevalence of part-time work in wholesale and retail trade and services, a switch from full- to part-time may help explain the large reemployment earnings losses. Half of workers reemployed in finance, insurance, and real estate experience no earnings loss or a gain, whereas the average change is a loss of 5.8 percent. Still, a sizable share of workers (about 30 percent) report losses greater than 30 percent. The median period of joblessness for these workers varies from 6 to 13 weeks, which again is consistent with the possibility that workers search first in manufacturing and, if unsuccessful, then turn to nonmanufacturing.

A small share of workers, about 5 percent, are reemployed in transportation and public utilities. This sector is highly unionized relative to the rest of the economy, with high average earnings. In comparison with other nonmanufacturing sectors, reemployment there also is associated with relatively small earnings losses (a median change of -1.0 percent and a mean change of -11.8 percent).

When we ask whether high import-competing displaced workers differ from other manufacturing workers in where they are reemployed, the answer is again clear: No. In the medium and low import-competing groups, 40 to 50 percent of workers return to manufacturing, with mean and median earnings losses smaller than 5 percent. These losses are markedly smaller than reemployment in nonmanufacturing industries. These similarities underscore the point that the proximate "cause" of job loss makes no difference in postdisplacement outcomes. What appears to matter is the kind of job lost and the kind of new job gained.

A few aspects of the low import-competing group stand out. This group contains both balanced and unbalanced exporters, along with some domestically oriented industries. About 43 percent of this group's reemployed return to manufacturing, with the median worker experiencing either no earnings loss or a small gain. Median jobless spells are just more than 1 month long, at 5 weeks.

For displaced manufacturing workers, construction provides a modest share of reemployment (4-6.5 percent). Median earnings losses are about 5 percent, and mean earnings losses are just under 10 percent, making the sector a possibly attractive option relative to other nonmanufacturing sectors.[2] Not only manufacturing workers return to their old sector. The high return percentages are seen most clearly among workers displaced from the nonmanufacturing sector—those displaced from utilities, wholesale and retail trade, and services. In large shares, these workers are reemployed in these same sectors. For transportation, utilities, and communications, the return percentage is 40 percent; for retail trade, 46 percent; for finance, insurance, and real estate, 47 percent. This is not surprising given the employment size and growth of these sectors. Many of these workers experience earnings gains, and if the average change is a loss, it is a small one. The small average earnings losses are consistent with the lower average earnings in nonmanufacturing sectors, as compared with manufacturing. We also know from the discussion in chapter 3 that these workers are more educated and have shorter tenure than manufacturing workers, and that is consistent with smaller earnings losses.

Sectoral Reemployment in More Detail

The percentages of workers reemployed in manufacturing may strike some as inconsistent with the notion that manufacturing employment is stagnant, if not in decline. There is no inconsistency. Half of manufacturing displaced workers return, and the other half are reemployed elsewhere in the economy. That is certainly consistent with a decline in employment opportunities in manufacturing. What is striking about those workers reemployed in manufacturing is the degree to which they are concentrated in the same set of industries from which they were displaced. Table 6.2 reports, for manufacturing workers, the detailed, 3-digit industries accounting for the largest shares of reemployment, across degrees of import competition.

There are two notable contrasts: Due to large employment size, the list of reemploying industries overlaps a great deal with the list of displacement industries (see table 2.1 and appendix table D.1). This overlap suggests little reallocation, in the sense that the industries with the biggest share of reemployment are the very same ones with large shares and numbers of displaced workers. For import-competing displaced workers, the largest reemployers—electrical machinery, apparel, motor vehicles, nonelectrical machinery—were the largest source of job loss. As a group, these reemployment shares show that vast numbers of import-competing displaced

---

2. Of the displaced manufacturing workers reemployed in construction, 92 percent are male.

Table 6.2 Industries accounting for largest shares of reemployment, by displaced industry level of import competition

Reemployment industry	High-import displaced		Medium-import displaced		Low-import displaced	
	Share	Median ln earnings change	Share	Median ln earnings change	Share	Median ln earnings change
High import-competing:						
Electrical machinery	0.069	0.006	0.018	−0.066		
Apparel and accessories	0.062	−0.047				
Motor vehicles	0.039	0.032	0.020	−0.117		
Electronic computing equipment[a]	0.026	−0.001				
Radio and television	0.025	0.105				
Medium import-competing:						
Machinery, except electrical[a]	0.026	−0.023	0.045	−0.023		
Furniture and fixtures			0.024	−0.023		
Aircraft[b]			0.017	−0.041		
Sawmills			0.020	−0.024		
Low import-competing:						
Newspaper publishing					0.016	−0.045
Printing, publishing[a]					0.084	0
Fabricated structural metals[a]					0.040	0.017
Nonmanufacturing:						
Construction	0.036	−0.086	0.065	0.053	0.049	0
Eating and drinking places	0.031	−0.301	0.028	−0.253	0.026	−0.466

a. Denotes "balanced" exporter.
b. Denotes "unbalanced" exporter.
Note: Shares and median earnings not reported for cells with fewer than 50 observations.
Source: Author's calculations from Displaced Worker Surveys, 1984-2000.

workers regain employment in the same industries where they lost their jobs. This suggests a high level of churning, where jobs are lost in some firms to import competition while the process of normal turnover in other firms continues to produce employment opportunities.

Yet, summed up, the actual share of workers reemployed in these large industries is quite small. This means that reemployment occurs in virtually every industry to some degree, suggesting considerable reallocation. In each of these industries, both reemployment shares and absolute numbers are small: 0.5 to 1 percent, or 30,000 to 60,000 workers.

The table also reports median earnings changes for the (weighted) set of workers reemployed in this limited set of industries. The main point from figures 6.1-6.3 also is in evidence here: Employment within the narrow set of old industries reduces earnings losses. Workers employed in electrical machinery and motor vehicles, at the median, earn as much or more on their new jobs as they did before displacement. Although speculative in nature, we can presume that these workers were displaced from jobs in these industries, and thus reemployment in the same industry minimizes earnings losses. Even import-competing displaced workers reemployed in apparel, a low-wage industry, experience relatively small earnings losses (4.7 percent). Such workers retain some part of the specific components of their earnings: their specific skills, union rents, efficiency wages, or positions in internal labor markets. The same pattern of reduced earnings losses (under 5 percent), with reemployment in a handful of manufacturing industries, is true across the board for displaced manufacturing workers.

Conversely, half of import-competing displaced workers are reemployed outside manufacturing. These workers are reemployed, in relatively small numbers, throughout wholesale and retail trade and services. Eating and drinking places represent the largest single reemploying industry, by share, and these workers suffer earnings losses in the range of 25 to 46 percent. This group represents about 10 percent of reemployed manufacturing workers, regardless of the level of import competition. This concentrated group of workers represents the clearest view of the costs of labor reallocation following import-competing job loss.

Looking further at reallocation, export-oriented manufacturing industries are only modestly represented among the largest reemploying industries. Table 6.2 indicates whether industries are balanced or unbalanced exporters, and despite some of considerable size, not much reemployment occurs there for import-competing displaced workers. Computers and machinery are the only reemploying industries of significant size that are exporters (yet also importers). A number of factors could play a role here: import-oriented industries tend to be in different geographical regions than export-intensive industries; workers in export-intensive industries have different observable characteristics from import-competing displaced workers (more workers have college degrees); and unobservable differences, such as the nature of the manufacturing processes (as in "new" manufacturing) might limit the ability of import-competing displaced workers to become reemployed in exporting industries.

Earlier displacement research encourages one more step, the consideration of reemployment in the same industry.[3] This research shows clearly that reemployment in the same industry is very important for reducing earnings losses. As shown in tables 6.1 and 6.2, same-industry reemployment is a minority outcome, but still a sizable minority. For manufacturing as a whole, about 19 percent of reemployed workers are back in the same 3-digit industry. Import-competing displaced workers are basically no

---

3. See Kletzer (1998b).

Table 6.3 Reemployment in the same detailed (3-digit) industry, by level of import competition

Level of import competition	Reemployed in same industry	
	No	Yes
High		
Number of workers	4,278,019	1,029,696
Share	0.806	0.194
Median earnings change	−0.0921	0
Mean earnings change	−0.1999	−0.019
Median weeks jobless	8.0	6.0
Medium		
Number of workers	4,948,143	1,049,606
Share	0.825	0.175
Median earnings change	−0.1059	−0.0214
Mean earnings change	−0.1863	−0.0066
Median weeks jobless	8.0	4.0
Low		
Number of workers	2,015,606	519,747
Share	0.795	0.205
Median earnings change	−0.0715	0
Mean earnings change	−0.1533	−0.079
Median weeks jobless	6.0	4.0
Nonmanufacturing		
Number of workers	16,598,400	5,801,600
Share	0.741	0.259
Median earnings change	−0.0155	0
Mean earnings change	−0.0709	−0.0372
Median weeks jobless	4.0	2.0

Note: Changes in earnings are changes in ln (earnings).

Source: Author's calculations from the Displaced Worker Surveys, 1984-2000.

more or less likely to be reemployed in the same industry as other manufacturing workers.

Table 6.3 reports the number, shares, and earnings changes for workers reemployed in or changing detailed industry. For all workers, a change of industry is associated with much larger earnings losses. Regaining employment in the same industry is associated with small or no earnings losses, at the median and the mean. For the import-competing displaced group, half of workers who return to the same industry report no earnings losses or a gain. Mean earnings losses are about 2 percent, about $8 a week for the average import-competing displaced worker using predisplacement earnings. At the same time, about 14 percent of high import-competing same-industry returnees report earnings losses greater than 30 percent. Reemployment in the same detailed industry does not guarantee that earnings will not be reduced, but it greatly reduces the average loss (from nearly 20 to 2 percent) and it greatly reduces the likelihood of very large earnings losses (from 34 to 15 percent).

The experience of workers who change 3-digit industry is very different. For the import-competing displaced group, half of all those who change industry have earnings losses greater than 10 percent, with the mean change a loss of 20 percent. If judged against old earnings, the loss is about $81 a week, or $4,200 a year. Thirty-four percent of these workers experience an earnings loss of more than 30 percent.

Larger earnings losses for those who change industry may not necessarily reflect solely the loss of specific skills. Other factors—such as efficiency wages, union wage premiums, incentive pay schemes, or internal labor markets—may also account for the earnings losses. It is somewhat difficult to separate the influence of a specific industry from the influence of remaining in manufacturing. For displaced manufacturing workers reemployed in manufacturing, average earnings losses are smaller for those who gain reemployment in the same 3-digit industry, relative to those who change industry. The mean earnings change for those who change manufacturing industry is −7.0 percent, and the mean earnings change for those who stay in a manufacturing industry is −2.5 percent.[4]

Who are the workers who return to the same industry? It is difficult to say much with confidence, because statistical models estimating the probability of returning to an industry have weak predictive power. There is some evidence that middle-aged workers with less formal schooling and longer job tenure are more likely to remain in their old industry. These are the very same worker characteristics that cause concern when we consider labor reallocation, because these are the workers who stand to lose specific components of earnings and for whom retraining may be difficult. Reemployment in the old sector looks to be the best outcome for expected earnings.

Implications for "Trade" and Labor Reallocation

These patterns of reemployment are both expected and perhaps unexpected. The patterns show both considerable reallocation and some maintenance of employment in old industries. They suggest a partial reallocation of labor, one that may be consistent with a short (1-3 year) horizon. It is not at all clear that a complete reallocation should be expected, given the presence of specific factors. The old sectors may be engaged in a form of long-term employment decline, but that process is not uniform across firms or industries. Production continues, normal

---

4. The one other study to do the same comparison reports different results. Jacobson, LaLonde, and Sullivan (1993) find for manufacturing workers that 6 years after separation, earnings losses are about the same (18-20 percent), with or without changes in 4-digit SIC industry, if reemployment is in the manufacturing sector.

turnover continues, and some employment opportunities remain open. For workers with specific skills, reestablishing a spot in manufacturing makes sense; it minimizes earnings losses. It also suggest avenues for reemployment efforts that do not involve formal (re)training. At the same time, the pattern of reemployment, particularly for manufacturing workers, shows that when workers are reallocated, it is at considerable cost.

These results also suggest that a uniform manufacturing-to-services view of labor reallocation is simplistic. Rather than thinking that entire industries are in decline, it is more realistic to think that some firms or activities in an industry decline while others start up or expand.[5]

This pattern is not a result of using a faulty definition of import-competing displacement. The working definition used here yields a set of industries that have faced consistently strong import competition. Import share is high and has risen, for the most part steadily, during the past 20 years. In addition, these industries overlap almost completely with the industries that account for most of the NAFTA-TAA certifications. These are not industries where the permanence of steady import competition is in question.

---

5. The variation within industries is best analyzed using firm- or establishment-level data. See Bernard and Jensen (1995) and the research summarized in Lewis and Richardson (2001).

7

Conclusions and Policy Implications: Addressing Costly Job Loss

The consequences of trade-related job loss for the domestic labor market are very likely the key political economy issue for the future of US international economic policy. Recent opinion surveys reveal that sizable majorities of Americans understand that the benefits of free trade are accompanied by costs, borne largely by workers who lose jobs (Scheve and Slaughter 2001). Considerable public opinion supports future trade agreements that address labor issues. In a recent poll, 78 percent of respondents answered that "protecting the jobs of American workers" should have top priority in deciding US policies about trading with other countries (see Pew Research Center for People and the Press 2000).

Trade liberalization is often a focal point for anxiety about job insecurity. That focus can be misplaced, in the sense that trade ranks behind technological change and immigration as a source of job loss and declining real wages for less educated workers. And there are also other sources of job loss: shifts in international investment, corporate restructuring, and changes in consumer demand. As the US economy slowed in late 2000 into 2001, announcements of job cutbacks were a regular feature in the business press. Yet even in good times there is a lot of job loss in the US economy. In 1999, when unemployment averaged 4.2 percent and 2.7 million new jobs were created, 2.5 million workers lost their jobs.

However unwelcome for some individuals, these changes bring clear, widespread benefits for the economy as a whole. And the relatively high job turnover in the United States brings benefits as well. Flexible labor markets facilitate the deployment of labor to growing sectors of the economy, where workers are much in demand and therefore highly valued.

Young workers particularly benefit from a flexible labor market, one where they can gain experience and skills, find ever better matches with employers, and realize higher earnings.

But the churning of labor markets—job losses and job gains—also has a downside. Losing a job can be a difficult and costly experience for an individual, and when large plants close, whole communities are affected adversely. Workers who retain their jobs through one stage of a plant closing or employment reduction may fear they will be next, with an attendant drop in morale.

In the midst of a rapidly changing labor market, Americans are wise to be anxious about losing jobs and wages. There is job loss associated with import competition, and this book has shown that job loss to be costly for the "average" (high) import-competing displaced manufacturing worker, with weekly earnings losses of about 13 percent.[1] These near-term earnings losses, though sizable, are exceeded by long-term losses. It is important to note that the large average earnings losses of import-competing workers are not significantly larger than those of manufacturing workers displaced for other reasons. This means that, with respect to the costs of job loss, "trade-displaced" manufacturing workers look little different from "otherwise-displaced" manufacturing workers. For all these workers, what matters is the kind of job lost and the kind of job regained, not why the job was lost.

Import-Competing Job Loss and Reemployment

But some characteristics of import-competing job loss make it different. Working in an import-competing industry does expose workers to a some-what higher risk of job loss. And these workers at risk, by their labor market and demographic characteristics, face real barriers to adjustment. Just 63 percent of import-competing displaced workers were reemployed when surveyed, and this percentage is consistently lower than that for manufacturing as a whole. We can understand and account for some of this difference when we take note of the characteristics of many import-competing manufacturing workers: slightly older, markedly less educated, with longer tenure. The evidence is clear: These individual characteristics are associated with a lower likelihood of reemployment.

The gender composition of import-competing employment and displacement also matters. The burden of import-competing displacement falls disproportionately on women, because they are heavily employed in many traditional import-competing industries. Women, particularly if

---

1. These estimated earnings losses do not account for lower earnings before the job is lost, nor income lost during unemployment.

married, tend to be much less likely to be reemployed after losing a job. These periods of joblessness increase the lifetime costs of job loss.

Age, education, and job tenure emerge as strong predictors of difficult readjustment. A middle-aged (or older), long-tenured, less educated worker may be ill prepared to enter a changed labor market. Although in many cases highly skilled for production work, he or she may be less flexible in adapting to new production techniques or not have the educational background to transfer to a well-paid service-economy job.

Although reemployment is a hurdle, particularly for import-competing displaced workers, the difficulties of job loss do not end when the new job is found. The lasting cost of job loss can be lower pay on the new job. And this cost is high for import-competing displaced workers, as it is for "otherwise displaced" manufacturing workers. Displaced manufacturing workers experience large earnings losses, on average 13 percent, as compared with a loss of 3.8 percent for displaced nonmanufacturing workers. Some of this difference in earnings change is explained by nonmanufacturing workers having characteristics associated with smaller earnings losses (or earnings gains), in ways different from manufacturing workers. In comparison with manufacturing workers, nonmanufacturing workers are likely to be younger, less tenured, college graduates, and white collar.

Large, persistent earnings losses make job dislocation costly for the "average" import-competing displaced worker. An equally important finding of this book is the considerable variation in earnings losses around the average: 35 percent of displaced manufacturing workers report earning the same or more on the new job as on the old one, whereas 25 percent report earnings losses of 30 percent or more. The distribution of earnings losses is virtually the same for otherwise displaced workers from manufacturing.

The industrial sector in which workers are reemployed goes a long way toward explaining the size and distribution of earnings losses. Among the reemployed, half of manufacturing displaced workers are reemployed in manufacturing. This outcome produces considerably smaller earnings losses. By extension, reemployment in the old industry is associated with the smallest earnings losses.

This reemployment within manufacturing is perhaps surprising and certainly noteworthy. It may also have important implications for the current training-based focus of displaced-worker assistance. The best outcome for many manufacturing workers—particularly those who are middle-aged and have less formal schooling and longer tenure—is (clearly) to return to their old industry. Their earnings losses will be smaller. With some job search assistance, this outcome may be quite feasible. It is interesting that this "reemployment in the old industry" outcome may also be why job search assistance appears cost-effective, because it helps workers look for jobs.[2] Tailoring that assistance in a way that helps workers seek reemployment where skills are most transferable is fully consistent with the patterns revealed in chapter 6.

There are other implications. One implicit premise of retraining efforts for displaced workers is the reallocation of workers to different jobs in various sectors of the economy. For this group of displaced workers, however, finding another job is very costly. Could training mitigate some of these reallocation earnings costs? Perhaps. The data used here offer no information that would allow an assessment of training. A substantial literature, however, reports the mixed results of training. There is ample evidence of the very high costs involved in retraining an adult unskilled laborer into a skilled worker (see Heckman 2000).

Current Compensation for Displaced Workers

Currently, the primary US program of assistance for unemployed workers is unemployment insurance. Unemployment insurance, introduced in the 1935 Social Security Act, is an essential federal policy tool. It helps cushion the income losses suffered by workers who lose jobs through no fault of their own. It also serves as an automatic fiscal stabilizer by providing supplemental income during a worker's period of unemployment that can help sustain aggregate consumption in the economy during times of overall economic weakness. The unemployment insurance system is a joint federal-state effort; the federal government establishes basic conditions and programs, and the states administer benefits. Funding comes from a payroll tax levied on employers, which is rated from experience to reflect differences in layoff rates.

The federal role in assisting "trade-displaced" workers began with the Trade Expansion Act of 1962. This act established the program of Trade Adjustment Assistance (TAA). Eligible workers for whom it can be documented that increasing imports have contributed importantly to their job loss, additional assistance is available. The size and form of TAA has changed considerably in the four decades since the passage of the Trade Expansion Act. Under its current form, qualified workers may gain an additional 52 weeks of income support (called Trade Readjustment Allowances), which is provided after they exhaust their unemployment compensation (which lasts 26 weeks) if they are enrolled in an approved training program. The program also provides job search and relocation assistance. Income-support payments are set at the prevailing state unemployment insurance benefit level. Although income-support payments under TAA are an entitlement, the other benefits, including training, are

---

2. See Leigh (1990).

limited by the availability of funds. The entire TAA program is funded out of general revenues.

Federal efforts to help trade-displaced workers were enhanced with the passage of the North American Free Trade Agreement Implementation Act of 1993, which created the North American Free Trade Agreement Transitional Adjustment Assistance (NAFTA-TAA) program. NAFTA-TAA is similar to TAA in general form, although it covers only workers who have lost jobs because of increased imports from—or shifts of production to—Canada or Mexico. Workers can be certified under both programs but must choose one from which to claim benefits. Benefits provided under NAFTA-TAA are identical to those provided under TAA. NAFTA-TAA also provides benefits to secondary workers, defined as those employed by upstream producers and/or suppliers. As with TAA, the federal government pays all NAFTA-TAA expenses. During the late 1990s, annual TAA and NAFTA-TAA service and benefit payments were less than $300 million.[3]

In 1999, the latest year for which information is available, 227,650 workers were certified as eligible for TAA and/or NAFTA-TAA.[4] Certifications include workers who lose jobs as well as those threatened with job loss. It is interesting to note that the number of 1999 certifications is close to a Displaced Worker Survey estimate of the number of workers displaced from high import-competing industries in 1999: 295,000. But only 36,910 workers received readjustment allowances, and only 32,120 received training. A US General Accounting Office report discussed reasons for low training enrollment, including training waivers (allowed under TAA but not under NAFTA-TAA), funding shortfalls, and a strong labor market that allowed displaced workers to become reemployed more readily on their own (US General Accounting Office 2000).

Evidence that TAA and NAFTA-TAA training programs are useful is weak, at best (see Decker and Corson 1995; US General Accounting Office 2000). Because workers typically enter training before getting a new job, there is a weak link between training and the skill needs of potential employers. This raises the possibility that workers may train for jobs that do not exist. But this is not to say that training has no value to anyone. Classroom training can be of real value to some dislocated workers, but the share who benefit is quite small.[5] Most workers acquire far more skill-enhancing knowledge on the job than in the classroom (see Jacobson 1998).

---

3. See US General Accounting Office (2000). This report is the source for the information that follows on certified workers.

4. This number includes workers certified under both programs.

5. This point is echoed in one of the observations from chapter 4: The value of more schooling (or training), in helping reemployment, depends on a worker's other characteristics and therefore is not the same for all workers.

Policy Implications

For policy, one of the most important conclusions of this book is that, for manufacturing, displaced workers and the consequences of their dislocations are more alike than different across the various reasons for job loss. If workers and consequences are alike, whatever the cause of job loss—including increasing foreign competition, technological change, shifts in international investment, and industrial restructuring—policymakers need to consider adjustment and assistance policies for all displaced workers, not just those displaced by trade.

A straightforward implication of the research reported here is that—because of the strong association between higher age, less formal education, long tenure, and difficult labor market adjustment—assistance programs need to target certain groups of workers, rather than provide the same services to all. This approach is in the spirit of the worker profiling used by states in providing reemployment services.[6]

The pattern of reemployment found in this study has implications for addressing some of the holes in the existing safety net for displaced workers. We know that job search assistance can be offered at low cost (see Leigh 1990). Enhanced, industry-specific search assistance could help (some) workers become reemployed in manufacturing, where their earnings losses would likely be minimized. This type of search assistance, focused on reemployment in the old industry, might make sense for the current generation of established workers in import-competing industries. For these workers, reemployment outside manufacturing produces large, persistent earnings losses—and (yet) the costs of retraining are high. The cost-effective approach may be to encourage reemployment where and for as long as job opportunities exist.

At the same time, reallocation to growing sectors of the economy can be costly for manufacturing workers. With society benefiting overall from the reallocation, these private costs deserve close consideration. The large, persistent earnings losses reported here and in other studies reveal the "real" costs of job loss: lower pay on the new job. These costs can be addressed directly by wage insurance (a program of financial assistance, upon reemployment) for workers who lose jobs, for any reason, through no fault of their own. The goal of wage insurance is to get workers back to work as soon as possible, while minimizing long-term earnings losses. A key aspect of this insurance—and the difference between it and other

---

6. A first wave of states implemented the Worker Profiling and Reemployment Services system in 1994. This program, now operating in all states, usually employs a statistical model to identify those unemployment insurance recipients who are most likely to exhaust their benefits. The goal is to refer these workers to special reemployment services early in their benefit period.

kinds of adjustment assistance—is the employment incentive created by making benefits conditional on reemployment.[7]

The basics of a wage insurance program are described in Kletzer and Litan (2001). In brief, the program would be open to all workers who could provide documentation that they were "displaced" according to criteria similar to the operational definition of displacement used by the Bureau of Labor Statistics in its Displaced Worker Surveys. This definition (discussed in chapter 2) includes plant closing or relocation, elimination of position or shift, and insufficient work. Given the evidence in this book that long-tenured workers experience larger earnings losses, eligibility could be made contingent on a minimum period of service on the old job. (The Kletzer-Litan proposal suggests a minimum of 2 years' tenure on the old job.) Workers reemployed in a new job that pays less than the old one (both old and new job earnings can be documented through employers' quarterly earnings reports filed with the states) would have a substantial portion of their lost earnings replaced, for up to 2 years following the date of initial job loss. For example, a displaced worker who once earned $40,000 a year, reemployed in a new job paying $30,000, would receive $5,000 a year, for a period from the time of reemployment to 2 years after the job loss. Annual payments could be capped, perhaps at $10,000.

Kletzer and Litan provide cost estimates, based on DWS data, for a number of program scenarios. One scenario—with a replacement rate of 50 percent of lost earnings, a $10,000 annual cap, and eligibility limited to workers whose previous and new jobs were full-time—would have cost about $3 billion in 1997, when the unemployment rate averaged 4.9 percent.[8]

Wage insurance addresses some of the criticisms leveled at TAA and NAFTA-TAA. First, the structure of the program, with benefits available only upon reemployment, presents an incentive for workers to find new jobs quickly. Second, workers' job search efforts may be broader, as entry-level jobs become more attractive when the earnings gap is reduced. Third, the program effectively subsidizes retraining on the job, where it is likely to be far more useful than in a separate program with uncertain reemployment prospects. Fourth, the program directly addresses the critical problem in evidence here: earnings losses upon reemployment.

In the policy arena, an additional cost of job displacement not addressed here is the loss of access to employer-subsidized health insurance. Kletzer

---

7. In the research literature, other proponents of wage insurance include Burtless et al. (1998) and Jacobson (1998).

8. Some of the cost of a wage insurance program could be offset if it were incorporated into the TAA and NAFTA-TAA programs. One possibility would be to offer wage insurance to workers if they became reemployed within 26 weeks, the period before the extended income support from Trade Readjustment Allowances. Once receiving wage insurance, reemployed workers would be ineligible for income support and training allowances.

and Litan advance a proposal for subsidized health insurance premiums for displaced workers during a limited period of unemployment. Although all laid-off workers now have a right to purchase unsubsidized health insurance from their former employer if it was offered when they were employed, many jobless workers cannot take advantage of this guarantee, due to the high cost of premiums and the loss of income during unemployment. If all full-time displaced workers were offered a 50 percent subsidy of their health insurance premium costs for a period up to 6 months or until they found a new job (whichever came first), the projected costs would be $750 million.[9]

Many American workers fear job loss and its consequences. This book reveals a small but significant group of workers for whom import-competing job loss is very costly. For other workers, realized costs are smaller. A knowledge of this range of outcomes should assist policymakers in targeting assistance to those who suffer the real costs of import-competing job loss.

Are import-competing displaced workers more deserving of assistance than other displaced manufacturing workers? The answer depends on the perspective used to define "deserving." This book finds that, for the most part, import-competing displaced workers experience outcomes similar to other manufacturing workers with similar skills. The identity of the old industry plays virtually no part in explaining the pattern of postdisplacement outcomes. This answer of "no" is based somewhat narrowly on the economics of the question. A more realistic, politically aware answer is that any notion that trade-displaced workers are special or more deserving is likely to come from the sense that explicit policy decisions, such as trade liberalization, are linked to the job loss. If these policy decisions confer benefits on the whole and losses on a concentrated few, then it may be in the interests of the whole to compensate the few, out of fairness and to allow the process to move forward. From these perspectives of equity and politics, the few are "deserving."

One reading of the globalization backlash is that the political process needs to better recognize the losers from free trade and the scope of their losses, and devise effective government mechanisms to ease the (necessary) labor market readjustments. There is an emerging consensus that future progress on trade liberalization may be conditioned on a more active domestic labor market policy agenda, including displaced worker adjustment policies. For example, members of the US Trade Deficit Review Commission (2000) were split in most of their findings and recommendations, largely on partisan lines. In their final report, their one area of unanimous agreement was advocating displaced worker adjustment policies (in particular wage insurance).

---

9. As in the wage insurance proposal, this cost projection for subsidized health insurance is based on 1997 labor market and eligibility parameters.

The past three decades of trade liberalization and economic integration have proceeded without much government involvement. Ending the policy stalemate is likely to require more government initiative. In a democratic society, the winners may well need to compensate the losers so that the political process can continue to generate trade liberalization. In a compassionate society, the winners should compensate the losers.

APPENDICES

Appendix A
Data on Trade Flows and Job Loss

To define a set of import-competing industries, the central data challenge involves bringing together product-based trade flows and production data with industry-based employment and job loss data.

Data on the value of US imports and exports, by 4-digit SIC category, are available as part of the NBER Trade Database for the period 1958-94. The data file also reports the 1958-94 value of domestic shipments from the NBER Productivity Database.[1] Import share is defined as the ratio of imports to total domestic supply, where total domestic supply is the sum of domestic production (shipments) minus exports plus imports.

The SIC-based industry trade data must be aggregated up to 3-digit 1990 CIC codes, to combine the trade information with information on job displacement based on the Current Population Survey.

Measuring Industry Job Loss Using the Current Population Survey

The Displaced Worker Surveys (DWSs) are administered biennially as supplements to the Current Population Survey. The CPS is a monthly survey of about 60,000 households that provides basic data on employment and unemployment for the United States. The first DWS

---

1. The 1958-94 file combines data from the earlier NBER Trade and Immigration data file (described in Abowd 1991) with the NBER Trade Database (see Feenstra 1996).

was administered in January 1984 and the most recent in February 2000. The time series of surveys provide coverage of displacements for the period 1979-99. In each survey, adults (aged 20 years and older) in the regular monthly CPS were asked if they had lost a job in the preceding 3- or 5-year period due to "a plant closing, an employer going out of business, a layoff from which he/she was not recalled, or other similar reasons."[2] If the answer was yes, a series of questions followed concerning the old job and the period of joblessness.

A common understanding of job displacement is that it occurs without personal prejudice; terminations are related to the operating decisions of the employer and are independent of individual job performance. In the DWSs, this definition can be implemented by drawing the sample of displaced from individuals who respond that their job loss was due to the reasons noted above. Other causes of job loss, such as quits or firings, are not considered displacements.[3] This operational definition is not without ambiguity: the displacements are "job" displacements, in the sense that an individual displaced from a job and rehired for a different job by the same employer is considered displaced.

Some of the distinctions may be too narrow or arbitrary. The distinction between quits and displacements is muddied by the ability of employers to reduce employment by reducing or failing to raise wages. Wage changes may induce some workers to quit (and not be in the sample), whereas others opt to stay with the firm (and they get displaced and enter the sample).[4] This distinction means that the displaced-worker sample will underestimate the amount of job change "caused" by trade. In addition, if the workers who stay on with the firm until displacement are those who face the worst labor market outcomes of all those at risk of displacement, then the displaced sample will be potentially nonrandom, and it will overstate the costs of job loss. Without data on quits, these issues cannot be addressed.

Defining the Sample

The sample here is limited to workers displaced from manufacturing industries, aged 20 to 64 years at the time of displacement. Because the information is retrospectively gathered, it has potential recall error. Prob-

---

2. For the 1984-92 surveys, the recall period was 5 years. Starting in 1994, the recall period was shortened to 3 years.

3. Individuals may also respond that their job loss was due to the end of a seasonal job or the failure of a self-employed business. These individuals are not considered displaced in this book. For a discussion of these reasons, see Farber (2001).

4. Jacobson, LaLonde, and Sullivan (1993) show that wages fall for displaced workers before they are displaced.

lems of recall are compounded by the overlapping coverage of years of displacement by surveys, with some years covered in two or three surveys.[5] This bias is believed to be significant. As Topel and Farber show, it is likely that the surveys seriously underestimate job loss that occurred long before the survey date due to inaccuracies in recall as well as question design.[6] This makes it desirable to have nonoverlapping recall periods (i.e., each year of displacement drawn from only one survey) that are relatively short. To incorporate these characteristics and to establish a count of displaced workers, the sample was restricted to displacements occurring in the 2-year period before each survey. A larger sample was drawn from the 1984 survey to extend the time series coverage back to 1979. Industry displacement rates, reported in table 2.1, were calculated by dividing the number of workers displaced from a 3-digit CIC industry in a year by the number of workers employed in that industry in that year.

To the extent that these procedures are used to establish a count of import-competing displaced workers, there are some limitations. Multiple job losses per worker are not counted. Respondents who report "other" as their reason for job loss are excluded. Using a 2-year window for the 1984-92 surveys (which had 5-year recall periods) will undercount job loss, because workers who report losing jobs in the fourth or fifth year before the survey will be counted as nonlosers. Farber (1997, 2001) adopts a correction method, which is not used here. Overall, my count should be considered a conservative one, but one that is systematically conservative across all industries. If I undercount job loss, I expect to do so across the board, not differentially by industry.

Once the count of displaced workers was established for table 2.1, the fullest sample of displaced workers was drawn from the DWSs to investigate worker characteristics and analyze postdisplacement outcomes.

---

5. The 1984 DWS covered the period 1979-83; the 1986 survey, 1981-85; the 1988 survey, 1983-87; the 1990 survey, 1985-89; the 1992 survey, 1987-91; the 1994 survey, 1991-93; and the 1996 survey, 1993-95.

6. If more than one job was lost, information is gathered only for the job held longest. See Topel (1990) and Farber (1997).

Appendix B
Intraindustry Trade

An industry's import share and export intensity provide a rough understanding of intraindustry trade, in the sense that high import share teamed with high export intensity suggest that the industry is actively importing and exporting. A more precise, now-established method for measuring intraindustry trade was offered by Grubel and Lloyd in 1975. That measure is:

$$IIT = 1 - \frac{|X - M|}{X + M}$$

where X and M represent, respectively, the value of exports and imports of an industry, and the vertical bars in the numerator denote the absolute value. The value of IIT ranges from 0, when an industry only exports or imports, to 1, when an industry's exports and imports are equal. Thus, the higher the value of IIT, the greater the degree of trade overlap, or intraindustry trade.

For our purposes, the Grubel-Lloyd index can be altered slightly to reveal not only whether trade is balanced, but also whether an industry is relatively more export oriented or import oriented. This is done simply by calculating the index without the absolute value. On the basis of these calculations, I can make a rough judgment as to whether an industry is an exporter or importer, and balanced or unbalanced.

Appendix C
Summary of Longitudinal Studies of Postdisplacement Earnings Changes

The Displaced Worker Surveys lack information on both long-term earnings changes and on how earnings would have grown if the displaced workers had not lost their jobs. However, studies using longitudinal data from national surveys and state administrative sources have provided useful insights on these issues.

On the basis of job losses in the early 1980s, Jacobson, LaLonde, and Sullivan (1993; hereafter, JLS) found large earnings losses following displacement, relative to what similar workers continued to earn when they stayed on their jobs, for a sample of Pennsylvania workers strongly attached to the labor market (prime-aged, with 6 or more years' job tenure before job loss and consistent attachment following). This comparison to a similar control group is critical and has been an important methodological approach to displaced-worker studies. Most important, earnings fell slightly in the year before separation. After the job loss, earnings fell sharply relative to the earnings of workers who remained with their firms for the next 4 years. Beyond 4 years, the earnings of displaced workers were nearly $2,000 a quarter less than their nonseparated counterparts.

JLS sharpen their focus on established workers when they identify a group of "mass layoff separators." These are workers who separate from firms where employment declined by more than 30 percent from a late-1970s peak. Although this group may be a minority of the displaced, it also likely includes workers for whom the employment relationship was

Parts of this appendix have been drawn from Lori G. Kletzer, 1998, Job Displacement, Journal of Economic Perspectives *(winter): 115-36. Reprinted with permission from the American Economic Association.*

valuable. This group may include those with low levels of formal schooling, high tenure, and in unionized jobs, similar to some of our group of import-competing displaced workers. For this group of mass-layoff separators, the first costs of displacement occur about 3 years before separation, when their quarterly earnings decline by $1,000 relative to expected earnings, due to hours reductions, real pay cuts, and temporary layoffs. After displacement, quarterly earnings of these workers fall by another $2,000 to $3,000 below expected levels. Even after 5 or 6 years, quarterly earnings remain between $1,000 and $2,000 below expected levels. These losses equal approximately 25 percent of predisplacement earnings. Similar patterns of earnings losses are found for this group across gender, age, and industrial sector, although the picture does vary to some extent according to the strength of the regional economy.

One limitation of the JLS analysis is its use of Pennsylvania data, because displacement in a traditional industrial state may not be representative of the nation as a whole. It is, however, likely to be fairly representative of a subset of our group of import-competing displaced workers. In a national sample of experienced displaced workers drawn from the Panel Survey on Income Dynamics, Stevens (1997) found large, persistent earnings losses. In her sample, annual earnings fall approximately 25 percent in the year before job displacement. One year after displacement, earnings remain 15 percent below the earnings of the nondisplaced, and are highly variable. The losses are persistent; during the period 7 or more years following job loss, annual earnings are 6-12 percent below expected levels. Annual earnings fall because of both a decline in hours and a decline in wages. One year before displacement, hourly wages decline 8 percent below expected levels, and 1 year following displacement they remain 12 percent below expected levels. The hourly earnings declines are also persistent: 7 years after job loss, average hourly earnings are approximately 9 percent below expected levels, and similar losses are found at 10 years after displacement.

One important finding in Stevens (see also Schoeni and Dardia 1996) is that the number of separations is an important component of long-term earnings losses. For example, 41 percent of Stevens's sample reports at least two job displacements during a 20-year sample period. Whereas average annual earnings reductions 6 years after job loss are approximately 12 percent, if only a single job loss has been suffered, average earnings losses are approximately 4 percent. These findings would be consistent with a pattern in which hourly wages fall significantly with the first job loss due to the loss of specific skills and rents, but wages do not fall much with subsequent job loss because workers are less likely to accumulate specific skills or earn rents on their postdisplacement jobs. Thus, multiple job losses reduce annual earnings further not because they reduce wages further, but instead because they make a reduction in future hours of employment more likely.

Appendix D
Tables

Table D.1 Manufacturing industries by degree of import competition, with trade and job loss measures, 1979-99

Industry	Total displaced, 1979-99	Share of total manufacturing displaced, 1979-99	Mean job loss rate, 1979-99	Change in import share 1979-94	Change in import share 1979-85	Change in import share 1985-94	1979 import Share	Change In exports 1979-94	Trade overlap mean, 1975-94 "Original"	Trade overlap mean, 1975-94 "Altered"	Importer or exporter? Balanced or unbalanced?
High import-competing											
Electrical machinery, I	1,576,095										
Electrical machinery	1,180,706	0.0703	0.0402	0.2063	0.0712	0.1351	0.1066	1.1721	0.8631	1.0904	Balanced importer
Radio, television	395,389	0.0235	0.1052	0.147	0.0458	0.1012	0.151	1.312	0.607	1.393	Unbalanced importer
Apparel, I											
Apparel	1,135,668	0.0676	0.0562	0.2497	0.1034	0.1464	0.1322	1.3434	0.1743	1.8257	Unbalanced importer
Transportation equipment, I	985,760										
Motor vehicles	918,066	0.0546	0.0431	0.1012	0.0857	0.0156	0.1733	0.7828	0.5403	1.4597	Unbalanced importer
Cycles and miscellaneous transport	67,694	0.0040	0.0838	-0.0631	-0.0221	-0.041	0.2906	0.9753	0.832	1.1413	Balanced importer
Machinery, except electrical, I	905,514										
Electronic computing equipment	513,988	0.0306	0.0454	0.384	0.086	0.298	0.1031	1.1805	0.8034	0.8892	Balanced exporter
Construction and material moving machines	350,900	0.0209	0.0526	0.1771	0.0905	0.0866	0.0595	-0.1908	0.5845	0.5845	Unbalanced exporter
Office and accounting machines	40,626	0.0024	0.0297	0.3715	0.0827	0.2888	0.0795	0.1494	0.7618	1.0752	Balanced importer
Metal, I	494,660										
Blast furnaces	361,428	0.0215	0.0531	0.0709	0.0739	-0.003	0.1191	0.017	0.3211	1.6789	Unbalanced importer
Other primary metal	133,232	0.0079	0.0719	0.0024	0.0222	-0.0198	0.189	-0.0474	0.782	1.1858	Balanced importer
Miscellaneous manufacturing industries	335,091	0.0199	0.0505	0.1902	0.1099	0.0803	0.1857	0.0331	0.4147	1.5853	Unbalanced importer
Leather and leather products	246,451										
Footwear	184,417	0.0110	0.0871	0.3587	0.2192	0.1395	0.3478	1.3752	0.0825	1.9175	Unbalanced importer
Leather products	57,337	0.0034	0.1217	0.3906	0.195	0.1957	0.2694	0.7729	0.1404	1.8596	Unbalanced importer
Leather tanning and finishing	4,697	0.0003	0.074	0.1173	0.0725	0.0448	0.16	0.5605	0.8868	0.9601	Balanced exporter

Professional and photographic equipment

240,200

Scientific and controlling instruments	163,503	0.0097	0.0278	0.154	0.0424	0.1116	0.0743	0.7092	0.6788	0.6788	Balanced exporter
Photographic equipment	67,754	0.0040	0.0321	0.1396	0.0519	0.0877	0.1206	0.0279	0.8045	1.1646	Balanced importer
Watches, clocks	8,943	0.0005	0.0913	0.4129	0.2261	0.1868	0.3873	−0.0476	0.156	1.844	Unbalanced importer

Rubber and miscellaneous plastics

192,960

Other rubber products	113,144	0.0067	0.0437	0.1567	−0.0125	0.1692	0.0861	0.8918	0.6539	1.3461	Unbalanced importer
Tires and inner tubes	79,816	0.0048	0.0452	0.096	0.038	0.058	0.1295	1.0439	0.4941	1.5059	Unbalanced importer

Textiles, I

159,177

Knitting mills	137,725	0.0082	0.0342	0.1585	0.0973	0.0612	0.0606	1.4413	0.2528	1.7472	Unbalanced importer
Miscellaneous textiles	21,452	0.0013	0.0449	0.0146	0.0142	0.0005	0.1186	0.7878	0.8867	1.083	Balanced importer
Toys and sporting goods	155,970	0.0093	0.0597	0.2781	0.148	0.1301	0.2292	1.0191	0.3386	1.6614	Unbalanced importer
Pottery and related	26,471	0.0016	0.0733	0.1326	0.1054	0.0271	0.3126	0.7543	0.3121	1.6879	Unbalanced importer
Totals/means	6,454,017	0.3842	0.0594	0.1846	0.0846	0.1000	0.1689	0.6984	0.5378	1.3637	Unbalanced importer

Medium import-competing

Machinery, except electrical, II

1,413,793

Machinery, except electrical	931,268	0.0554	0.0408	0.102	0.0521	0.0499	0.0845	0.5445	0.8855	0.9451	Balanced exporter
Metalworking machinery	254,338	0.0151	0.0351	0.1287	0.0611	0.0677	0.1077	0.4878	0.8162	1.181	Balanced importer
Farm machinery and equipment	147,914	0.0088	0.0636	0.0329	0.0193	0.0137	0.1252	0.1583	0.8808	0.9767	Balanced exporter
Engines and turbines	80,273	0.0048	0.0423	0.1061	0.1128	−0.0067	0.083	0.5415	0.7114	0.751	Balanced exporter

Transportation equipment, II

984,854

Aircraft and parts	366,443	0.0218	0.0276	0.1316	0.0341	0.0975	0.0447	0.6899	0.3928	0.3928	Unbalanced exporter
Ship and boat building	339,632	0.0202	0.0658	0.0214	0.018	0.0034	0.0188	0.865	0.6012	0.7518	Balanced exporter
Guided missiles	226,226	0.0135	0.0684	0.048	0.0183	0.0297	0.0086	0.073	0.7609	0.7711	Unbalanced exporter
Railroad locomotives	52,553	0.0031	0.1074	0.0887	0.0627	0.026	0.0527	0.0112	0.7829	0.9563	Balanced exporter

(table continues next page)

Table D.1 Manufacturing industries by degree of import competition, with trade and job loss measures, 1979-99
(continued)

Industry	Total displaced, 1979-99	Share of total manufacturing displaced, 1979-99	Mean job loss rate, 1979-99	Change in import share 1979-94	1979-85	1985-94	1979 import share	Change In exports 1979-94	Trade overlap mean, 1975-94 "Original"	"Altered"	Importer or exporter? Balanced or unbalanced?
Metal, II	849,720										
Miscellaneous fabricated metals	340,304	0.0203	0.0314	0.0453	0.0193	0.026	0.0398	0.5936	0.8628	1.0939	Balanced importer
Iron and steel foundries	139,257	0.0083	0.0477	0.0298	0.0236	0.0062	0.0165	0.2704	0.6109	1.3891	Unbalanced importer
Metal forgings	107,463	0.0064	0.0317	0.0213	0.0164	0.0048	0.021	-0.7482	0.8335	0.886	Balanced exporter
Primary aluminum industries	96,387	0.0057	0.0624	0.1093	0.0451	0.0641	0.0479	0.6637	0.7827	1.1399	Balanced importer
Cutlery, handtools	86,086	0.0051	0.0338	0.1034	0.0441	0.0593	0.0731	0.7123	0.7487	1.2503	Unbalanced importer
Ordnance	49,842	0.0030	0.0628	0.1119	0.0026	0.1093	0.0406	0.1247	0.6098	0.6098	Balanced exporter
Screw machine products	30,381	0.0018	0.028	0.067	0.0176	0.0494	0.0887	1.13	0.5002	1.4998	Unbalanced importer
Food and kindred products	562,591										
Canned fruit	208,685	0.0124	0.0339	0.0163	0.0233	-0.007	0.038	0.7416	0.8055	1.1899	Balanced importer
Miscellaneous foods	192,143	0.0114	0.0407	0.0172	0.0061	0.0111	0.0492	-0.1151	0.6439	0.6439	Unbalanced exporter
Beverages	96,663	0.0058	0.0207	-0.0033	0.0024	-0.0058	0.0713	1.0538	0.3641	1.6359	Unbalanced importer
Sugar products	65,100	0.0039	0.038	-0.0619	-0.0313	-0.0306	0.1394	1.3732	0.5955	1.403	Unbalanced importer
Furniture and fixtures	550,404	0.0328	0.0257	0.0866	0.0485	0.0381	0.0464	1.4756	0.4117	1.5883	Unbalanced importer
Chemicals and allied products, I	510,528										
Industrial and miscellaneous chemicals	286,703	0.0171	0.0297	0.0615	0.0404	0.0211	0.0709	0.3493	0.743	0.743	Balanced exporter
Drugs	132,952	0.0079	0.0261	0.0414	0.0117	0.0297	0.0516	1.0641	0.7521	0.7521	Balanced exporter
Plastics, synthetics	90,873	0.0054	0.0254	0.0806	0.0241	0.0564	0.0235	0.6076	0.4656	0.4656	Unbalanced exporter
Miscellaneous plastic products	391,773	0.0233	0.0417	0.0438	0.0126	0.0312	0.0319	1.0348	0.8747	1.0359	Balanced importer
Textiles, II	335,375										
Yarn, thread	298,764	0.0178	0.0375	0.0623	0.0405	0.0218	0.0453	0.0567	0.7215	1.2559	Balanced importer
Floor coverings	36,611	0.0022	0.0476	0.0236	0.022	0.0016	0.0466	0.7201	0.795	1.1969	Balanced importer
Sawmills, planing mills	313,622	0.0187	0.0362	0.0084	0.0029	0.0055	0.1353	0.4065	0.6376	1.3624	Unbalanced importer
Optical and health supplies	279,636	0.0166	0.1095	0.0515	0.0082	0.0433	0.0636	1.3681	0.8075	0.8075	Balanced exporter
Glass and glass products	154,257	0.0092	0.0488	0.0736	0.038	0.0356	0.0555	0.6607	0.8248	1.1539	Balanced importer
Household appliances	150,142	0.0089	0.0481	0.0967	0.0502	0.0465	0.0711	0.6025	0.7361	1.2337	Balanced importer

Industry	Employment										Trade assessment
Miscellaneous fabricated textiles	147,324	0.0088	0.0395	0.1085	0.0434	0.0651	0.0397	0.1624	0.5924	1.3807	Unbalanced importer
Miscellaneous wood products	117,380	0.0070	0.0405	0.0354	0.0136	0.0218	0.0659	0.7257	0.5789	1.4211	Unbalanced importer
Miscellaneous nonmetallic minerals	97,085	0.0058	0.0449	0.0656	0.0386	0.027	0.0465	0.4672	0.869	1.091	Balanced importer
Pulp, paper	95,859	0.0057	0.0194	0.0135	0.004	0.0095	0.1548	0.6439	0.7937	1.2063	Balanced importer
Petroleum refining	88,234	0.0053	0.0293	0.0101	0.0256	−0.0156	0.0751	0.817	0.4422	1.5578	Unbalanced importer
Miscellaneous petroleum	19,853	0.0012	0.0717	0.0221	0.0243	−0.0022	0.0497	−0.1881	0.7111	1.2361	Balanced importer
Structural clay products	13,970	0.0008	0.0835	0.0876	0.0323	0.0553	0.0917	−0.3327	0.461	1.539	Balanced importer
Totals/means	7,076,400	0.4212	0.0622	0.0564	0.0278	0.0286	0.0626	0.5355	0.6867	1.0944	
Low import-competing	1,091,687										
Printing, publishing, and allied industries											
Printing, publishing	868,641	0.0517	0.036	0.008	0.0022	0.0058	0.0133	0.9694	0.7207	0.7207	Balanced exporter
Newspaper	223,046	0.0133	0.0226	−0.0008	0.0019	−0.0028	0.0012	1.1193	0.5948	1.2425	Unbalanced importer
Food and kindred products, II	610,132										
Meat products	260,861	0.0155	0.0304	−0.014	−0.0084	−0.0056	0.0479	0.7099	0.8574	0.913	Balanced exporter
Bakery	130,075	0.0077	0.0285	0.0085	0.0045	0.004	0.0053	2.0603	0.5856	1.4144	Unbalanced importer
Dairy products	114,393	0.0068	0.0441	0.0017	0.0007	0.0009	0.015	1.0272	0.8149	1.1745	Balanced importer
Grain milling	104,803	0.0062	0.0359	0.0132	0.0027	0.0105	0.0053	0.1336	0.2335	0.2335	Unbalanced exporter
Fabricated structural metals	537,044	0.0320	0.0528	0.009	0.0088	0.0002	0.0072	−0.0295	0.6309	0.6309	Balanced exporter
Cement, concrete, gypsum	154,755	0.0092	0.0306	−0.0084	0.0061	−0.0145	0.0207	0.3969	0.465	1.535	Unbalanced importer
Paperboard	153,757	0.0092	0.0329	0.009	0.003	0.0061	0.0037	1.487	0.7287	0.7287	Balanced exporter
Soaps and cosmetics	139,046	0.0083	0.0386	0.0299	0.0113	0.0186	0.0092	1.223	0.7143	0.7143	Balanced exporter
Miscellaneous paper	132,406	0.0079	0.0315	0.0103	0.0094	0.0009	0.0142	0.9942	0.7481	0.7915	Balanced exporter
Wood and mobile buildings	110,757	0.0066	0.0872	−0.0123	0.0002	−0.0125	0.047	0.1074	0.3461	1.6539	Unbalanced importer
Logging	74,905	0.0045	0.0504	0.0101	−0.0042	0.0143	0.0104	0.0272	0.086	0.086	Unbalanced exporter
Paints, varnishes	40,198	0.0024	0.0504	0.0141	0.0065	0.0076	0.002	1.0552	0.4005	0.4005	Unbalanced exporter
Tobacco	17,796	0.0011	0.0664	0.0004	−0.0017	0.0021	0.0071	1.2397	0.2333	0.2333	Unbalanced exporter
Totals/means	3,062,483	0.1823	0.0425	0.0052	0.0028	0.0023	0.0139	0.8347	0.5439	0.8315	

Note: See text for an explanation of the balanced/unbalanced trade assessment. Industries are defined at the 3-digit CIC level; some industries are grouped together at the 2-digit CIC level (in bold).

Source: Author's calculations from the Displaced Worker Surveys and the National Bureau of Economic Research Trade Database.

Table D.2 Characteristics of displaced workers

Panel A, 1979-99

Worker characteristics	High import compe-tition, manufac-turing	Medium import compe-tition, manufac-turing	Low import compe-tition, manufac-turing	All manufac-turing	Utilities, trade, services
Age at displacement (years)					
20-24	0.131	0.149	0.157	0.144	0.164
25-34	0.323	0.338	0.340	0.333	0.344
35-44	0.267	0.240	0.262	0.254	0.256
45-54	0.174	0.169	0.155	0.168	0.153
55-64	0.104	0.103	0.087	0.101	0.082
Mean age, years (standard deviation)	39.1	38.4	37.8	38.6	37.3
	(11.4)	(11.6)	(11.3)	(11.5)	(11.2)
Education					
Less than high school	0.213	0.219	0.182	0.210	0.119
High school graduate	0.427	0.444	0.446	0.437	0.365
Some college	0.212	0.210	0.229	0.215	0.294
College degree or higher	0.148	0.126	0.142	0.137	0.222
Mean years of education	12.3	12.3	12.5	12.3	13.2
(standard deviation)	(2.7)	(2.6)	(2.5)	(2.6)	(2.4)
Job tenure at time of displacement (years)					
Less than 3	0.388	0.398	0.442	0.402	0.510
3-5	0.221	0.231	0.230	0.227	0.229
6-10	0.168	0.154	0.134	0.156	0.133
11-20	0.130	0.133	0.125	0.131	0.082
Greater than 20	0.091	0.083	0.069	0.084	0.045
Mean job tenure, years	6.8	6.5	5.9	6.5	4.6
(standard deviation)	(7.9)	(7.8)	(7.7)	(7.8)	(6.2)
Share female	0.449	0.304	0.351	0.369	0.504
Share minority	0.190	0.165	0.167	0.176	0.170
Share displaced from fulltime jobs	0.966	0.960	0.924	0.956	0.837
Predisplacement occupation					
White collar	0.313	0.286	0.345	0.307	0.645
Skilled blue collar	0.180	0.209	0.155	0.188	0.075
Unskilled blue collar	0.488	0.478	0.466	0.480	0.138
Services	0.018	0.025	0.029	0.023	0.140
Weekly earnings on the old job					
Mean (standard deviation)	$402.97	$400.41	$375.11	$396.88	$368.65
	($273.39)	($236.55)	($230.52)	($250.89)	($269.19)
Share earned less than $200/week	0.24	0.16	0.18	0.18	0.28
Share earned more than $800/week	0.07	0.06	0.05	0.06	0.07
Share reemployed at survey date	0.634	0.654	0.668	0.648	0.691
For reemployed					
Mean change in log earnings	−0.132	−0.126	−0.086	−0.121	−0.038
	(0.475)	(0.469)	(0.475)	(0.473)	(0.575)
Median change in log earnings	−0.047	−0.062	−0.027	−0.047	0
Share with no earnings loss or earning more	0.36	0.34	0.38	0.35	0.41
Share with earnings losses greater than 15 percent	0.35	0.36	0.34	0.35	0.29
Share with earnings losses greater than 30 percent	0.25	0.25	0.26	0.25	0.21

Table D.2 *(continued)*

Panel B, 1979-89

Worker characteristics	High import competition, manufacturing	Medium import competition, manufacturing	Low import competition, manufacturing	All manufacturing	Utilities, trade, services
Age at displacement (years)					
20-24	0.153	0.177	0.178	0.167	0.198
25-34	0.351	0.364	0.354	0.357	0.370
35-44	0.248	0.207	0.234	0.228	0.224
45-54	0.145	0.149	0.149	0.148	0.127
55-64	0.102	0.103	0.084	0.099	0.080
Mean age, years (standard deviation)	38.5	37.8	37.5	38.1	36.6
	(11.6)	(11.8)	(11.5)	(11.7)	(11.3)
Education					
Less than high school	0.226	0.250	0.199	0.232	0.145
High school graduate	0.459	0.477	0.467	0.469	0.419
Some college	0.189	0.164	0.196	0.179	0.249
College degree or higher	0.125	0.108	0.137	0.120	0.186
Mean years of education	12.1	11.9	12.3	12.1	12.9
(standard deviation)	(2.6)	(2.6)	(2.6)	(2.6)	(2.4)
Job tenure at time of displacement (years)					
Less than 3	0.413	0.429	0.465	0.429	0.563
3-5	0.221	0.229	0.225	0.225	0.219
6-10	0.156	0.145	0.134	0.148	0.112
11-20	0.133	0.125	0.119	0.127	0.072
Greater than 20	0.072	0.071	0.056	0.071	0.034
Mean job tenure, years	6.4	6.0	5.5	6.1	4.1
(standard deviation)	(7.7)	(7.5)	(7.1)	(7.5)	(5.8)
Share female	0.443	0.305	0.340	0.367	0.478
Share minority	0.160	0.151	0.144	0.154	0.136
Share displaced from full-time jobs	0.965	0.960	0.929	0.956	0.859
Predisplacement occupation					
White collar	0.281	0.256	0.331	0.279	0.614
Skilled blue collar	0.188	0.214	0.165	0.195	0.092
Unskilled blue collar	0.509	0.499	0.467	0.498	0.165
Services	0.022	0.029	0.037	0.028	0.129
Weekly earnings on the old job					
Mean (standard deviation)	$397.69	$391.82	$366.97	$389.96	$360.84
	($245.80)	($217.23)	($205.57)	($227.62)	($249.57)
Share earned less than $200/week	0.25	0.16	0.17	0.18	0.26
Share earned more than $800/week	0.06	0.05	0.04	0.05	0.06
Share reemployed at survey date	0.623	0.652	0.652	0.640	0.670
For reemployed					
Mean change in log earnings	−0.144	−0.125	−0.072	−0.123	−0.027
	(0.476)	(0.452)	(0.465)	(0.465)	(0.522)
Median change in log earnings	−0.072	−0.077	−0.021	−0.068	0
Share with no earnings loss or earning more	0.39	0.40	0.46	0.41	0.50
Share with earnings losses greater than 15 percent	0.36	0.36	0.32	0.35	0.28
Share with earnings losses greater than 30 percent	0.26	0.26	0.24	0.25	0.20

(table continues next page)

Table D.2 Characteristics of displaced workers *(continued)*

Panel C, 1990-99

Worker characteristics	High import compe- tition, manufac- turing	Medium import compe- tition, manufac- turing	Low import compe- tition, manufac- turing	All manufac- turing	Utilities, trade, services
Age at displacement (years)					
20-24	0.094	0.105	0.126	0.105	0.135
25-34	0.275	0.298	0.320	0.294	0.322
35-44	0.299	0.294	0.301	0.297	0.284
45-54	0.224	0.200	0.162	0.202	0.175
55-64	0.108	0.103	0.091	0.102	0.083
Mean age, years	40.2	39.4	38.3	39.5	37.9
(standard deviation)	(11.1)	(11.2)	(11.0)	(11.2)	(11.0)
Education					
Less than high school	0.190	0.170	0.157	0.175	0.097
High school graduate	0.369	0.389	0.417	0.387	0.318
Some college	0.254	0.286	0.277	0.272	0.332
College degree or higher	0.186	0.155	0.149	0.166	0.252
Mean years of education	12.7	12.7	12.8	12.7	13.5
(standard deviation)	(2.8)	(2.6)	(2.4)	(2.7)	(2.3)
Job tenure at time of displacement (years)					
Less than 3	0.345	0.349	0.409	0.359	0.466
3-5	0.221	0.233	0.237	0.229	0.237
6-10	0.190	0.168	0.134	0.169	0.150
11-20	0.127	0.146	0.133	0.136	0.091
Greater than 20	0.116	0.103	0.087	0.105	0.055
Mean job tenure, years	7.4	7.2	6.5	7.2	5.1
(standard deviation)	(8.3)	(8.2)	(8.5)	(8.3)	(6.5)
Share female	0.460	0.303	0.366	0.374	0.526
Share minority	0.242	0.189	0.201	0.222	0.199
Share displaced from full-time jobs	0.969	0.961	0.917	0.956	0.819
Predisplacement occupation					
White collar	0.369	0.334	0.365	0.353	0.672
Skilled blue collar	0.167	0.199	0.140	0.176	0.060
Unskilled blue collar	0.452	0.444	0.464	0.451	0.115
Services	0.010	0.017	0.018	0.015	0.149
Weekly earnings on the old job					
Mean (standard deviation)	$412.67	$414.82	$387.29	$408.68	$375.80
	($317.67)	($265.23)	($263.03)	($285.81)	($285.78)
Share earned less than $200/week	0.25	0.17	0.20	0.21	0.28
Share earned more than $800/week	0.90	0.09	0.06	0.08	0.07
Share reemployed at survey date	0.654	0.657	0.691	0.663	0.708
For reemployed					
Mean change in log earnings	−0.110	−0.130	−0.106	−0.118	−0.046
	(0.472)	(0.496)	(0.489)	(0.486)	(0.617)
Median change in log earnings	−0.021	−0.046	−0.042	−0.036	−0.0044
Share with no earnings loss or earning more	0.45	0.40	0.42	0.42	0.49
Share with earnings losses greater than 15 percent	0.32	0.35	0.37	0.34	0.310
Share with earnings losses greater than 30 percent	0.24	0.25	0.29	0.26	0.22

Note: Workers displaced from agriculture, mining, construction, forestry, and fishing were excluded.

Source: Author's calculations from the Displaced Worker Surveys, 1984-2000, using sampling weights.

Table D.3 Characteristics of "medium" import-competing industry workers, rank ordered by number of workers displaced, 1979-99

Industry	Mean old job earnings	Share female	Share high school Dropouts	Share high school Graduates	Share with tenure > 10 years	Share reemployed	Change in weekly earnings Median	Change in weekly earnings Mean	Share with earnings loss > 30 percent	Share with joblessness > 26 weeks
Machinery, except electrical	$418.78	0.206	0.166	0.484	0.203	0.697	-0.037	-0.147	0.245	0.225
Furniture and fixtures	$318.99	0.318	0.334	0.428	0.181	0.623	-0.043	-0.087	0.224	0.191
Miscellaneous plastic products	$331.29	0.364	0.281	0.467	0.16	0.644	-0.079	-0.146	0.223	0.21
Aircraft and parts	$534.97	0.276	0.132	0.399	0.197	0.67	-0.214	-0.281	0.321	0.269
Miscellaneous fabricated metal	$366.98	0.271	0.157	0.521	0.243	0.633	-0.137	-0.202	0.273	0.274
Ship and boat building	$402.05	0.104	0.237	0.491	0.21	0.665	-0.095	-0.316	0.289	0.303
Sawmills, planing mills	$335.35	0.124	0.315	0.449	0.192	0.72	-0.029	-0.07	0.204	0.244
Yarn, thread	$289.84	0.518	0.356	0.428	0.257	0.664	-0.077	-0.174	0.29	0.241
Industrial and miscellaneous chemicals	$508.54	0.228	0.13	0.395	0.222	0.755	-0.092	-0.254	0.271	0.238
Optical and health supplies	$443.62	0.491	0.141	0.299	0.105	0.696	-0.037	-0.108	0.206	0.182
Metalworking machinery	$442.98	0.192	0.116	0.509	0.217	0.74	-0.041	-0.149	0.251	0.301
Guided missiles	$616.11	0.286	0.046	0.267	0.277	0.654	-0.177	-0.335	0.332	0.163
Canned fruit	$341.58	0.421	0.329	0.363	0.225	0.535	-0.048	-0.06	0.161	0.258
Miscellaneous foods	$312.72	0.526	0.333	0.439	0.181	0.512	-0.026	-0.135	0.268	0.211
Glass and glass products	$405.66	0.36	0.208	0.483	0.412	0.668	-0.124	-0.293	0.302	0.24
Household appliances	$360.77	0.482	0.252	0.539	0.277	0.52	-0.119	-0.325	0.32	0.33
Farm machinery and equipment	$416.08	0.225	0.147	0.54	0.259	0.634	-0.259	-0.31	0.39	0.378
Miscellaneous fabricated textiles	$215.67	0.762	0.327	0.499	0.174	0.605	0	0.157	0.21	0.263
Iron and steel foundries	$356.39	0.131	0.345	0.483	0.26	0.591	-0.103	-0.191	0.342	0.458
Drugs	$510.98	0.532	0.078	0.296	0.27	0.731	-0.134	-0.258	0.3	0.142
Miscellaneous wood products	$247.75	0.382	0.3	0.453	0.114	0.639	0	-0.067	0.207	0.275
Metal forgings	$363.79	0.293	0.226	0.493	0.265	0.536	-0.087	-0.157	0.293	0.258
Miscellaneous nonmetallic mineral	$439.68	0.168	0.263	0.422	0.254	0.647	-0.048	-0.129	0.23	0.178
Beverages	$429.80	0.285	0.171	0.42	0.206	0.668	-0.089	-0.132	0.228	0.279
Primary aluminum industries	$458.64	0.187	0.11	0.558	0.327	0.489	-0.143	-0.248	0.303	0.421
Pulp, paper	$519.34	0.278	0.122	0.502	0.231	0.624	-0.141	-0.196	0.278	0.147
Plastics, synthetics	$396.61	0.419	0.118	0.432	0.239	0.766	-0.128	-0.164	0.353	0.1

(table continues next page)

Table D.3 Characteristics of "medium" import-competing industry workers, rank ordered by number of workers displaced, 1979-99 (continued)

Industry	Mean old job earnings	Share female	Share high school Dropouts	Share high school Graduates	Share with tenure > 10 years	Share reemployed	Change in weekly earnings Median	Change in weekly earnings Mean	Share with earnings loss > 30 percent	Share with joblessness > 26 weeks
Petroleum refining	$671.35	0.186	0.202	0.299	0.295	0.715	-0.136	-0.15	0.337	0.238
Cutlery, handtools	$357.18	0.42	0.215	0.447	0.106	0.58	-0.038	-0.208	0.269	0.284
Engines and turbines	$443.01	0.202	0.137	0.496	0.3	0.766	-0.093	-0.105	0.228	0.334
Sugar products	$277.30	0.605	0.381	0.423	0.227	0.497	-0.149	-0.228	0.272	0.338
Not specified manufacturing	$216.68	0.296	0.322	0.454	0.254	0.533	0.075	0.245	0	0.108
Railroad locomotives	$490.86	0.137	0.259	0.463	0.367	0.728	-0.365	-0.561	0.474	0.416
Ordnance	$435.66	0.289	0.14	0.419	0.24	0.683	-0.202	-0.25	0.33	0.231
Agricultural chemicals	$391.14	0.079	0.298	0.402	0.075	0.777	-0.121	0.012	0.076	0.254
Floor coverings	$264.63	0.46	0.264	0.59	0.373	0.688	-0.137	-0.288	0.355	0.198
Screw machine products	$380.52	0.214	0.372	0.446	0.235	0.693	-0.076	-0.087	0.194	0.149
Dyeing textiles	$236.71	0.419	0.249	0.441	0.045	0.663	0	0.072	0.065	0.273
Miscellaneous petroleum	$372.96	0.423	0.262	0.461	0.14	0.405	-0.288	-0.099	0.379	0.188
Not specified electrical machinery	$243.86	0.492	0.14	0.38	0.146	0.546	0.014	0.032	0	0.343
Structural clay products	$511.71	0.227	0.235	0.342	0.134	0.411	-0.262	-0.099	0.28	0.459
Medium import-competing average	$400.41	0.304	0.219	0.444	0.216	0.654	-0.062	-0.126	0.253	0.246
Manufacturing average	$396.88	0.369	0.211	0.437	0.215	0.648	-0.047	-0.121	0.252	0.15
Nonmanufacturing average	$368.65	0.511	0.119	0.365	0.127	0.691	0	-0.038	0.212	0.251

Note: Changes in weekly earnings are changes in ln (earnings). See table 3.4 and appendix table D.4 for high and low import-competing industries.

Source: Author's calculations from the Displaced Worker Surveys, 1984-2000, using Current Population Survey sampling weights.

Table D.4 Characteristics of low import-competing industry workers, rank ordered by number of workers displaced, 1979-99

Industry	Mean old job earnings	Share female	Share high school Dropouts	Share high school Graduates	Share with tenure > 10 years	Share reemployed	Change in weekly earnings Median	Change in weekly earnings Mean	Share with earnings loss > 30 percent	Share with joblessness > 26 weeks
Printing, publishing	$385.24	0.487	0.092	0.419	0.157	0.67	-0.048	-0.209	0.269	0.197
Fabricated structural metals	$380.48	0.166	0.199	0.484	0.183	0.695	0	-0.123	0.288	0.206
Meat products	$312.18	0.379	0.287	0.48	0.202	0.665	-0.188	-0.216	0.331	0.276
Newspaper	$314.99	0.559	0.033	0.327	0.148	0.734	0.075	0.012	0.181	0.252
Cement, concrete, gypsum	$421.56	0.148	0.229	0.442	0.239	0.613	-0.155	-0.25	0.351	0.242
Paperboard	$354.53	0.362	0.267	0.455	0.193	0.633	-0.143	-0.206	0.286	0.169
Soaps and cosmetics	$385.74	0.527	0.204	0.497	0.274	0.523	-0.082	-0.253	0.279	0.241
Miscellaneous paper	$396.29	0.36	0.213	0.467	0.211	0.687	0.003	-0.255	0.264	0.317
Bakery	$325.72	0.388	0.256	0.448	0.227	0.641	-0.028	-0.21	0.254	0.194
Dairy products	$380.05	0.228	0.19	0.521	0.298	0.626	-0.083	-0.257	0.319	0.27
Wood and mobile buildings	$303.18	0.209	0.356	0.466	0.042	0.75	-0.13	-0.088	0.243	0.145
Grain milling	$392.37	0.257	0.169	0.369	0.345	0.692	-0.021	-0.03	0.231	0.218
Logging	$445.42	0.086	0.35	0.441	0.171	0.649	-0.078	-0.131	0.242	0.176
Paints, varnishes	$441.91	0.282	0.148	0.419	0.425	0.671	-0.007	-0.077	0.17	0.202
Tobacco	$480.61	0.303	0.196	0.641	0.449	0.59	0.155	-0.223	0.151	0.324
Low import-competing average	$375.11	0.351	0.182	0.446	0.194	0.668	-0.027	-0.086	0.251	0.219
Manufacturing average	$396.88	0.369	0.211	0.437	0.215	0.648	-0.047	-0.121	0.252	0.15
Nonmanufacturing average	$368.65	0.511	0.119	0.365	0.127	0.691	0	-0.038	0.212	0.251

Note: Changes in weekly earnings are changes in ln (earnings). See table 3.4 and appendix table D.3 for high and medium import-competing industries.

Source: Author's calculations from the Displaced Worker Surveys, 1984-2000, using Current Population Survey sampling weights.

Table D.5 Coefficient estimates from logit estimation of survey date employment, full sample

Characteristic	(1)	(2)	(3)
Manufacturing (nondurable goods)	−0.2715**	−0.1262*	−0.1242**
	(0.0879)	(0.0589)	(0.0481)
Manufacturing (durable goods)	−0.1313*	−0.1043*	−0.1955**
	(0.0590)	(0.0456)	(0.0433)
Transportation, communications, utilities	−0.0443	−0.0122	−0.1197
	(0.0804)	(0.0671)	(0.0658)
Age at displacement (years)			
20-24		0.4330**	0.3932**
		(0.0498)	(0.0507)
25-34		0.5053**	0.4857**
		(0.0361)	(0.0364)
35-44		0.5095**	0.5084*
		(0.0448)	(0.0455)
Education			
High school graduate		0.4872**	0.5156*
		(0.0366)	(0.0376)
Some college		0.7367**	0.7490*
		(0.0378)	(0.0390)
College degree or higher		1.1490**	1.1241*
		(0.0416)	(0.0421)
Job tenure (years)			
Less than 3		0.0489	0.0880
		(0.0477)	(0.0489)
3-5		0.1734**	0.2139*
		(0.0464)	(0.0481)
6-10		0.1353**	0.1689*
		(0.0478)	(0.0489)
Displaced from full-time job		0.4693**	0.3605*
		(0.0436)	(0.0419)
Minority		−0.4895**	−0.4751*
		(0.0378)	(0.0381)
Married		0.0891**	0.0538
		(0.0323)	(0.0310)
Female			−0.4494*
			(0.0283)
Year displaced			
1979-80	−0.3471**	−0.3442**	−0.3400*
	(0.0689)	(0.0726)	(0.0704)
1984-89	0.2583**	0.2480**	0.2617*
	(0.0390)	(0.0378)	(0.0380)
1990-92	0.2318**	0.1686**	0.1771*
	(0.0395)	(0.0415)	(0.0413)
1993-99	0.8058**	0.7911**	0.8190*
	(0.0430)	(0.0438)	(0.0446)
Years since displacement	0.3763**	0.3658**	0.3716*
	(0.0165)	(0.0176)	(0.0175)
Constant	−0.4137**	−1.8051**	−1.5017*
	(0.0587)	(0.0944)	(0.0971)
Observations	35,435	35,222	35,222

*significant at 5 percent; **significant at 1 percent.

Note: Robust standard errors in parentheses.

Table D.6 Coefficient estimates from logit estimation of survey date employment, manufacturing sample

Characteristic	(1)	(2)	(3)	(4)
High import-competing	−0.1789*	−0.1528**	−0.0912	−0.0917
	(0.0854)	(0.0547)	(0.0573)	(0.0591)
Medium import-competing	−0.0296	0.0009	−0.0134	−0.0176
	(0.0700)	(0.0623)	(0.0557)	(0.0559)
Age at displacement (years)				
20-24		0.4755**	0.4184**	0.4733**
		(0.0929)	(0.0909)	(0.0924)
25-34		0.5291**	0.4974**	0.5265**
		(0.0607)	(0.0607)	(0.0598)
35-44		0.4937**	0.4831**	0.5003**
		(0.0807)	(0.0824)	(0.0825)
Education				
High school graduate		0.4646**	0.4712**	0.4844**
		(0.0523)	(0.0531)	(0.0540)
Some college		0.6443**	0.6171**	0.6160**
		(0.0564)	(0.0569)	(0.0588)
College degree or higher		1.2019**	1.1327**	1.1281**
		(0.0727)	(0.0768)	(0.0774)
Job tenure (years)				
Less than 3		0.1868**	0.2553**	0.2752**
		(0.0596)	(0.0621)	(0.0632)
3-5		0.2849**	0.3496**	0.3712**
		(0.0663)	(0.0684)	(0.0700)
6-10		0.2887**	0.3362**	0.3546**
		(0.0618)	(0.0614)	(0.0626)
Displaced from full-time job		0.4942**	0.3628**	0.3209**
		(0.1306)	(0.1351)	(0.1336)
Minority		−0.4917**	−0.4542**	−0.4690**
		(0.0597)	(0.0614)	(0.0616)
Married		0.1719**	0.1259**	0.4745**
		(0.0438)	(0.0429)	(0.0636)
Female			−0.4649**	0.0104
			(0.0495)	(0.0605)
Female × married				−0.7854**
				(0.1174)
Year displaced				
1979-80	−0.4238**	−0.4331**	−0.4207**	−0.4248**
	(0.0948)	(0.1053)	(0.1012)	(0.1002)
1984-89	0.2998**	0.3212**	0.3301**	0.3352**
	(0.0537)	(0.0515)	(0.0528)	(0.0549)
1990-92	0.2412**	0.2154**	0.2179**	0.2190**
	(0.0588)	(0.0614)	(0.0588)	(0.0597)
1993-99	0.7896**	0.8205**	0.8431**	0.8583**
	(0.0687)	(0.0750)	(0.0757)	(0.0780)
Years since displacement	0.4133**	0.4137**	0.4172**	0.4164**
	(0.0224)	(0.0249)	(0.0255)	(0.0254)
Constant	−0.6097**	−2.1699**	−1.8902**	−2.1190**
	(0.0841)	(0.1639)	(0.1542)	(0.1566)
Observations	13,846	13,795	13,795	13,795

*significant at 5 percent; **significant at 1 percent.

Note: Robust standard errors in parentheses.

References

Abowd, John M. 1991. The NBER Immigration, Trade, and Labor Markets Data Files. In *Immigration, Trade and the Labor Market*, eds. J. M. Abowd and R. B. Freeman, 407-22. Chicago: University of Chicago Press.

Aho, C. Michael, and James A. Orr. 1979. *International Trade and Domestic Employment: Characteristics of Workers in Trade-Sensitive Industries*. Washington: Bureau of International Labor Affairs, US Department of Labor.

Aho, C. Michael, and James A. Orr. 1981. Trade-Sensitive Employment: Who Are the Affected Workers? *Monthly Labor Review* 104, no. 2: 29-35.

Bednarzik, Robert W. 1993. Analysis of U.S. Industries Sensitive to International Trade. *Monthly Labor Review* 116, no. 2: 15-31.

Bernard, Andrew B., and J. Bradford Jensen. 1995. Exporters, Jobs and Wages in U.S. Manufacturing: 1976-1987. *Brookings Papers on Economic Activity: Microeconomics*: 67-119.

Blanchflower, David G. 2000. Globalization and the Labor Market. Paper commissioned by US Trade Deficit Review Commission, Washington (September).

Borjas, George J., Richard B. Freeman, and Lawrence F. Katz. 1992. On the Labor Market Effects of Immigration and Trade. In *Immigration and the Work Force: Economic Consequences for the United States and Source Areas*, eds. George J. Borjas and Richard B. Freeman. Chicago: University of Chicago Press.

Borjas, George J., Richard B. Freeman, and Lawrence F. Katz. 1997. How Much Do Immigration and Trade Affect Labor Market Outcomes? *Brookings Papers on Economic Activity* 1: 1-90.

Burtless, Gary, Robert Z. Lawrence, Robert E. Litan, and Robert J. Shapiro. 1998. *Globaphobia: Confronting Fears about Open Trade*. Washington: Brookings Institution.

Carrington, William J. 1993. Wage Losses for Displaced Workers: Is It Really the Firm that Matters? *Journal of Human Resources* 28, no. 3: 435-62.

Committee for Economic Development, Research and Policy. 2001. *From Protest to Progress: Addressing Labor and Environmental Conditions Through Free Trade*. Washington.

Corson, Walter, and Walter Nicholson. 1981. Trade Adjustment Assistance for Workers: Results of a Survey of Recipients under the Trade Act of 1974. In *Research in Labor Economics*, vol. 4, ed. Ronald Ehrenberg. Greenwich, CT: JAI Press.

Decker, Paul T., and Walter Corson. 1995. International Trade and Worker Displacement: Evaluation of the Trade Adjustment Assistance Program. *Industrial and Labor Relations Review* 48, no. 4: 758-74.

Dewald, William G. 1978. *The Impact of International Trade and Investment on Employment.* Washington: Bureau of International Labor Affairs, US Department of Labor.

Economic Policy Institute. 2001. *NAFTA at Seven: Its impact on workers in all three nations.* Washington: Economic Policy Institute.

Fallick, Bruce C. 1993. The Industrial Mobility of Displaced Workers. *Journal of Labor Economics* 11, no. 2: 302-23.

Fallick, Bruce C. 1996. A Review of the Recent Empirical Literature on Displaced Workers. *Industrial and Labor Relations Review* 50, no. 1: 5-16.

Farber, Henry S. 1997. The Changing Face of Job Loss in the United States, 1981-1995. *Brookings Papers on Economic Activity: Microeconomics*: 55-142.

Farber, Henry S. 2001. Job Loss in the United States, 1981-1999. Industrial Relations Section, Princeton University, Princeton, NJ. Photocopy (January).

Feenstra, Robert C. 1996. *U.S. Imports, 1972-1994: Data and Concordances.* NBER Working Paper 5515. Cambridge, MA: National Bureau of Economic Research.

Field, Alfred J., and Edward M. Graham. 1997. Is There a Special Case for Import Protection for the Textile and Apparel Sectors Based on Labour Adjustment? *The World Economy* 20, no. 2: 137-57.

Grubel, H.G., and P.J. Lloyd. 1975. *Intra-Industry Trade: The Theory and Measurement of International Trade in Differentiated Products.* London: Macmillan.

Haveman, Jon D. 1998. The Influence of Changing Trade Patterns on Displacements of Labor. *International Trade Journal* 12, no. 2: 259-92.

Heckman, James J. 2000. Policies to Foster Human Capital. *Research in Labor Economics* 54, no. 1: 3-56.

Hipple, Steven. 1999. Worker Displacement in the Mid-1990s. *Monthly Labor Review*, July: 15-32.

Hufbauer, Gary C., and Jeffrey J. Schott. 1993. *NAFTA: An Assessment* (revised edition). Washington: Institute for International Economics.

Jacobson, Louis. 1998. Compensation Programs. In *Imports, Exports, and the American Worker*, ed. Susan M. Collins. Washington: Brookings Institution.

Jacobson, Louis, Robert LaLonde, and Daniel Sullivan. 1993. *The Costs of Worker Dislocation.* Kalamazoo, MI: W.E. Upjohn Institute for Employment Research.

Kletzer, Lori G. 1989. Returns to Seniority after Permanent Job Loss. *American Economic Review* 79, no. 3: 536-43.

Kletzer, Lori G. 1992. Industrial Mobility Following Job Displacement: Evidence from the Displaced Worker Surveys. *Proceedings of 44th Annual Meeting of Industrial Relations Research Association*, January: 621-29.

Kletzer, Lori G. 1995a. Gender Differences in the Incidence and Consequences of Job Displacement from Import-Sensitive Industries. Santa Cruz, CA: University of California, Santa Cruz. Photocopy (September).

Kletzer, Lori G. 1995b. White Collar Job Displacement, 1983-91. Industrial Relations Research Association, *Proceedings of 47th Annual Meeting of Industrial Relations Research Association*, January: 98-107.

Kletzer, Lori G. 1996. The Role of Sector-Specific Skills in Post-Displacement Earnings. *Industrial Relations* 35, no. 4: 473-90.

Kletzer, Lori G. 1998a. International Trade and Job Loss in U.S. Manufacturing, 1979-91. In *Imports, Exports, and the American Worker*, ed. Susan M. Collins. Washington: Brookings Institution.

Kletzer, Lori G. 1998b. Job Displacement. *Journal of Economic Perspectives*, Winter: 115-36.

Kletzer, Lori G. 2000. Trade and Job Loss in U.S. Manufacturing, 1979-94. In *The Impact of International Trade on Wages*, ed. Robert C. Feenstra. Chicago: University of Chicago Press.

Kletzer, Lori G. 2001. Imports, Exports, and Jobs: What does trade mean for employment and job loss? W.E. Upjohn Institute for Employment Research, Kalamazoo, MI. Photocopy (July).

Kletzer, Lori G., and Robert W. Fairlie. 2001. The Long-Term Consequences of Job Displacement for Young Adult Workers. University of California, Santa Cruz, CA. Photocopy (January).

Kletzer, Lori G., and Robert E. Litan. 2001. Prescription to Relieve Worker Anxiety. International Economics Policy Brief PB01-2. Washington: Institute for International Economics.

Korenman, Sanders, and David Neumark. 1991. Does Marriage Really Make Men More Productive? Journal of Human Resources 26, no. 2: 282-307.

Korenman, Sanders, and David Neumark. 1992. Marriage, Motherhood, and Wages. Journal of Human Resources 27, no. 2: 233-55.

Kruse, Douglas L. 1988. International Trade and the Labor Market Experience of Displaced Workers. Industrial and Labor Relations Review 41, no. 3: 402-17.

Leigh, Duane E. 1990. Does Training Work for Displaced Workers? A Survey of Existing Evidence. Kalamazoo, MI: W.E. Upjohn Institute for Employment Research.

Levinsohn, James, and Wendy Petropoulos. 2000. Creative Destruction or Just Plain Destruction? The U.S. Textile and Apparel Industries since 1992. University of Michigan, Ann Arbor. Photocopy (November).

Lewis, Howard, and J. David Richardson. 2001. Why Global Commitment Really Matters! Washington: Institute for International Economics. Forthcoming.

Lovely, Mary E., and J. David Richardson. 2000. Trade Flows and Wage Premiums: Does Who or What Matter? In The Impact of International Trade on Wages, ed. Robert C. Feenstra. Chicago: University of Chicago Press.

Neal, Derek. 1995. Industry-Specific Human Capital: Evidence from Displaced Workers. Journal of Labor Economics 13, no. 4: 653-77.

Neumann, George R. 1978. The Labor Market Adjustments of Trade Displaced Workers: The Evidence from the Trade Adjustment Assistance Program. In Research in Labor Economics, vol. 4, ed. Ronald Ehrenberg. Greenwich, CT: JAI Press.

Pew Research Center for People and the Press. 2000. Doubts about China, Concerns about Jobs: Post-Seattle Support for the WTO. Philadelphia. Photocopy (March).

Powers, Laura, and Ann Markusen. 1999. A Just Transition? Lessons from Defense Worker Adjustment in the 1990s. Economic Policy Institute Technical Paper no. 237 (April). Washington: Economic Policy Institute.

Program on International Policy Attitudes. 2000. Americans on Globalization: A Study of U.S. Public Attitudes. College Park, MD. Photocopy (28 March).

Revenga, Ana L. 1992. Exporting Jobs? The Impact of Import Competition on Employment and Wages in U.S. Manufacturing. Quarterly Journal of Economics 107, no. 1: 255-84.

Richardson, J. David, and Karin Rindal. 1995. Why Exports Really Matter! Washington: Institute for International Economics and The Manufacturing Institute.

Richardson, J. David, and Karin Rindal. 1996. Why Exports Matter: More! Washington: Institute for International Economics and The Manufacturing Institute.

Ruhm, Christopher J. 1991. Are Workers Permanently Scarred by Job Displacements? American Economic Review 81, no. 1: 319-24.

Sachs, Jeffrey D., and Howard J. Shatz. 1994. Trade and Jobs in U.S. Manufacturing. Brookings Papers on Economic Activity: 1-69.

Sachs, Jeffrey D., and Howard J. Shatz. 1998. International Trade and Wage Inequality in the United States: Some New Results. In Imports, Exports, and the American Worker, ed. Susan M. Collins. Washington: Brookings Institution.

Scheve, Kenneth F., and Matthew J. Slaughter. 2001. Globalization and the Perceptions of American Workers. Washington: Institute for International Economics.

Schoeni, Robert F., and Michael Dardia. 1996. Wage Losses of Displaced Workers in the 1990s. RAND, Santa Monica, CA. Photocopy (September).

Schoepfle, Gregory K. 1982. Imports and Domestic Employment: Identifying Affected Industries. *Monthly Labor Review* 105, no. 8: 13-26.

Seitchik, Adam. 1991. Who Are Displaced Workers? In *Job Displacement: Consequences and Implications for Policy*, ed. John T. Addison. Detroit: Wayne State University Press.

Seitchik, Adam, and Jeffrey Zornitsky. 1989. *From One Job to the Next: Worker Adjustment in a Changing Labor Market*. Kalamazoo, MI: W. E. Upjohn Institute for Employment Research.

Slaughter, Matthew, and Bruce Blonigen. 2000. U.S. Skill Upgrading and Inward Foreign Direct Investment. *Review of Economics and Statistics* 83, no. 2: 362-76.

Stevens, Ann Huff. 1997. Persistent Effects of Job Displacement: The Importance of Multiple Job Losses. *Journal of Labor Economics* 15, no. 1: 165-88.

Topel, Robert. 1990. Specific Capital and Unemployment: Measuring the Costs and Consequences of Job Loss. *Carnegie-Rochester Conference Series on Public Policy* 33 (Autumn): 181-214.

US Department of Labor. 1994. *Report on the American Workforce*. Washington: US Government Printing Office.

US Department of Labor. 1995. *Report on the American Workforce*. Washington: US Government Printing Office.

US General Accounting Office. 2000. *Trade Adjustment Assistance: Trends, Outcomes, and Management Issues in Dislocated Worker Programs*. GAO-01-59. Washington: GAO.

US Trade Deficit Review Commission. 2000. *The U.S. Trade Deficit: Causes, Consequences, and Recommendations for Action*. Washington: US Trade Deficit Review Commission.

Index

unemployment compensation sources, 80-81
electrical machinery
    defining import-competing industry, 17
    exports, 23
    manufacturing overview, 11, 22
    questions and answers overview, 3
    reemployment pattern by sector, 70, 71-72
electronic computing equipment
    exports, 23, 24
    manufacturing overview, 10, 22
    reemployment pattern by sector, 72
employment
    manufacturing overview, 9-11, 20-22
    and trade balance, 24-26
    trade effects on, 11-12
    worker characteristic comparisons, 31
engines and turbines, manufacturing overview, 10
ethnic minority groups. See minority groups
exports
    data source descriptions, 89
    employment effects of, 11
    and import-competing industries, 18-19t, 22-26, 98-101t
    and intraindustry trade, 93
    manufacturing overview, 9-11
    questions and answers overview, 4-5
    reemployment pattern by sector, 72
    research overview, 7, 14

farm machinery and equipment
    exports, 24
    manufacturing overview, 10
finance sector, reemployment pattern by sector, 69, 70
footwear
    defining import-competing industry, 16, 17
    manufacturing overview, 10
    questions and answers overview, 3
    worker characteristic comparisons, 37, 40
full-time workers
    earnings loss comparisons, 56-57, 59
    reemployment pattern by sector, 69
    reemployment probability estimates, 45-46, 48, 49, 108t, 109t
    worker characteristic comparisons, 29t, 34t, 40, 102-04t

gender. See also women
    earnings loss comparisons, 56, 59
    questions and answers overview, 4
    reemployment pattern by sector, 70n
    reemployment probability estimates, 45, 48, 51
    research conclusions, 78-79
globalization
    costs overview, 1-2
    policy implications, 84
    research overview, 6-7
gross domestic product (GDP), imports and exports as share of, 9-10
Grubel-Lloyd trade overlap index, 23, 93

health insurance subsidies, 83-84
high import-competing industries
    compensation for displaced workers, 81
    defining, 16-17, 98-99t
    earnings loss comparisons, 59, 60t
    exports, 22-25
    job displacement, 18-19t, 21
    reemployment pattern by sector, 63-69, 64f, 68t, 71t, 73t
    reemployment probability estimates, 49-52, 50t, 109t
    research conclusions, 78
    research overview, 13
    worker characteristic comparisons, 33-40, 34t, 36t, 38-39t, 102-04t
hours worked. See full-time workers; part-time workers
human capital. See also specific aspects
    earnings loss comparisons, 55-57, 61
    worker characteristic comparisons, 28

import-competing industries, defining, 3, 15-22, 18-19t, 20f, 89-91, 98-101t. See also specific industries and categories
import-competing job loss, 9-26. See also specific aspects
    data source descriptions, 3, 13-15, 33, 89-91, 95-96
    defining industries, 7, 15-22, 18-19t, 20f, 89-91, 98-101t
    defining job loss, 3, 12-13, 90
    earnings loss comparisons, 55-62
    employment and exports as factors, 11-12, 22-26
    manufacturing overview, 9-11
    measuring imports, exports, and job loss, 14-15, 89-90
    policy implications, 6, 77, 82-85

exports, 24
worker characteristic comparisons, 40
logit models, described, 43n
low import-competing industries
  defining, 16, 101t
  exports, 25
  reemployment pattern by sector, 65,
    67f, 68t, 69-70, 71t, 73t
  reemployment probability estimates,
    49, 51
  research overview, 13
  worker characteristic comparisons, 33-
    35, 34t, 36, 36t, 40, 102-04t, 107t

machinery. *See also specific categories*
  exports, 24
  manufacturing overview, 10
  reemployment pattern by sector, 72
manufacturing. *See also specific industries
    and categories*
  defining import-competing industry,
    18-19t, 98-101t
  earnings loss comparisons, 58t, 59-61,
    60t
  overview of, 9-11, 20-22
  policy implications, 82, 84
  questions and answers overview, 2-5
  reemployment pattern by sector, 65-75,
    68t
  reemployment probability estimates,
    44t, 45-52, 50t, 108t, 109t
  research conclusions, 78-79
  research overview, 2, 6-7, 12-14
  worker characteristic comparisons, 27-
    41, 29t, 34t, 36t, 102-04t
marital status
  earnings loss comparisons, 58t, 59, 60t
  reemployment probability estimates,
    44t, 46, 49, 50t, 51-52, 108t, 109t
  research conclusions, 79
Mass Layoffs Statistics (MLS), 21
medium import-competing industries
  defining, 16-17, 20, 99-101t
  earnings loss comparisons, 60t
  exports, 24-25
  reemployment pattern by sector, 65,
    66f, 68t, 69, 71t, 73t
  reemployment probability estimates,
    49, 50t, 51, 109t
  research overview, 13
  worker characteristic comparisons, 33-
    36, 34t, 36t, 40, 102-04t, 105-06t
metals. *See also specific categories*

defining import-competing industry,
  17
manufacturing overview, 10
other primary, defining import-
  competing industry, 16, 17
minority groups
  earnings loss comparisons, 58t, 59, 60t
  questions and answers overview, 4
  reemployment probability estimates,
    44t, 45-50, 50t, 52, 108t, 109t
  worker characteristic comparisons, 28,
    29t, 34t, 102-04t
motor vehicles
  defining import-competing industry,
    16, 17
  exports, 23, 24n
  manufacturing overview, 10, 22
  questions and answers overview, 3
  reemployment pattern by sector, 70,
    71-72

National Bureau of Economic Research
  (NBER) databases, 14, 89
nondurable goods
  earnings loss comparisons, 58t, 59
  questions and answers overview, 4
  reemployment pattern by sector, 65-66
  reemployment probability estimates,
    44t, 45, 48, 51, 108t
nonelectrical machinery
  exports, 23
  questions and answers overview, 3
  reemployment pattern by sector, 70
nonmanufacturing. *See also specific
    industries*
  questions and answers overview, 4
  reemployment pattern by sector, 68t,
    69-70, 71t, 72, 73t
  research conclusions, 79
  research overview, 7-8
  worker characteristic comparisons, 27-
    33, 29t
North American Free Trade Agreement
  (NAFTA), 2n
North American Free Trade Agreement
  Implementation Act of 1993, 81
North American Free Trade Agreement-
  Transitional Adjustment Assistance
  (NAFTA-TAA) certifications
  and benefits provision, 81
  defining trade-related job loss, 12-13
  industry composition of, 17, 20, 20f
  reemployment pattern by sector, 75
  and wage insurance, 83n

wood buildings and mobile homes, manufacturing overview, 10
worker adjustment programs. *See also specific types*
policy implications, 6, 83-84
questions and answers overview, 2, 5
worker characteristic comparisons, 33
worker characteristics, 27-41. *See also specific characteristics*
high import-competing industry workers, 33-40, 34*t*, 36*t*, 38-39*t*, 102-04*t*
import-competing compared with other manufacturing workers, 33-40, 34*t*, 36*t*, 38-39*t*, 102-04*t*
longitudinal study data, 15, 95-96
low import-competing industry workers, 107*t*
manufacturing compared with nonmanufacturing workers, 28-33, 29*t*

medium import-competing industry workers, 105-06*t*
outcomes after job loss, 31-33
questions and answers overview, 2-5
research conclusions, 78-79
research overview, 6-8, 27-28
summary, 40-41
Worker Profiling and Reemployment Services system, 82*n*
worker reallocation. *See also specific sectors*
industry mobility studies, 61-62
policy implications, 82
questions and answers overview, 5
reemployment pattern by sector, 63-75
research conclusions, 80
worker skills. *See* job-search skills; job skills

yarn and threads, defining import-competing industry, 17

BOOKS

IMF Conditionality* John Williamson, editor
1983 ISBN 0-88132-006-4
Trade Policy in the 1980s* William R. Cline, editor
1983 ISBN 0-88132-031-5
Subsidies in International Trade*
Gary Clyde Hufbauer and Joanna Shelton Erb
1984 ISBN 0-88132-004-8
International Debt: Systemic Risk and Policy
Response* William R. Cline
1984 ISBN 0-88132-015-3
Trade Protection in the United States: 31 Case
Studies* Gary Clyde Hufbauer, Diane E. Berliner,
and Kimberly Ann Elliott
1986 ISBN 0-88132-040-4
Toward Renewed Economic Growth in Latin
America* Bela Balassa, Gerardo M. Bueno, Pedro-
Pablo Kuczynski, and Mario Henrique Simonsen
1986 ISBN 0-88132-045-5
Capital Flight and Third World Debt*
Donald R. Lessard and John Williamson, editors
1987 ISBN 0-88132-053-6
The Canada-United States Free Trade Agreement:
The Global Impact*
Jeffrey J. Schott and Murray G. Smith, editors
1988 ISBN 0-88132-073-0
World Agricultural Trade: Building a Consensus*
William M. Miner and Dale E. Hathaway, editors
1988 ISBN 0-88132-071-3
Japan in the World Economy*
Bela Balassa and Marcus Noland
1988 ISBN 0-88132-041-2
America in the World Economy: A Strategy for
the 1990s* C. Fred Bergsten
1988 ISBN 0-88132-089-7
Managing the Dollar: From the Plaza to the
Louvre* Yoichi Funabashi
1988, 2d ed. 1989 ISBN 0-88132-097-8
United States External Adjustment and the World
Economy* William R. Cline
May 1989 ISBN 0-88132-048-X
Free Trade Areas and U.S. Trade Policy*
Jeffrey J. Schott, editor
May 1989 ISBN 0-88132-094-3
Dollar Politics: Exchange Rate Policymaking in
the United States*
I. M. Destler and C. Randall Henning
September 1989 ISBN 0-88132-079-X
Latin American Adjustment: How Much Has
Happened?* John Williamson, editor
April 1990 ISBN 0-88132-125-7
The Future of World Trade in Textiles and
Apparel* William R. Cline
1987, 2d ed. June 1990 ISBN 0-88132-110-9

Completing the Uruguay Round: A Results-
Oriented Approach to the GATT Trade
Negotiations* Jeffrey J. Schott, editor
September 1990 ISBN 0-88132-130-3
Economic Sanctions Reconsidered (2 volumes)
Economic Sanctions Reconsidered: Supplemental
Case Histories
Gary Clyde Hufbauer, Jeffrey J. Schott, and
Kimberly Ann Elliott
1985, 2d ed. Dec. 1990 ISBN cloth 0-88132-115-X
ISBN paper 0-88132-105-2
Economic Sanctions Reconsidered: History and
Current Policy
Gary Clyde Hufbauer, Jeffrey J. Schott, and
Kimberly Ann Elliott
December 1990 ISBN cloth 0-88132-140-0
ISBN paper 0-88132-136-2
Pacific Basin Developing Countries: Prospects for
the Future* Marcus Noland
January 1991 ISBN cloth 0-88132-141-9
ISBN 0-88132-081-1
Currency Convertibility in Eastern Europe*
John Williamson, editor
October 1991 ISBN 0-88132-128-1
International Adjustment and Financing: The
Lessons of 1985-1991* C. Fred Bergsten, editor
January 1992 ISBN 0-88132-112-5
North American Free Trade: Issues and
Recommendations*
Gary Clyde Hufbauer and Jeffrey J. Schott
April 1992 ISBN 0-88132-120-6
Narrowing the U.S. Current Account Deficit*
Allen J. Lenz
June 1992 ISBN 0-88132-103-6
The Economics of Global Warming
William R. Cline/*June 1992* ISBN 0-88132-132-X
U.S. Taxation of International Income: Blueprint
for Reform* Gary Clyde Hufbauer, assisted by
Joanna M. van Rooij
October 1992 ISBN 0-88132-134-6
Who's Bashing Whom? Trade Conflict in High-
Technology Industries Laura D'Andrea Tyson
November 1992 ISBN 0-88132-106-0
Korea in the World Economy* Il SaKong
January 1993 ISBN 0-88132-183-4
Pacific Dynamism and the International Economic
System*
C. Fred Bergsten and Marcus Noland, editors
May 1993 ISBN 0-88132-196-6
Economic Consequences of Soviet Disintegration*
John Williamson, editor
May 1993 ISBN 0-88132-190-7
Reconcilable Differences? United States-Japan
Economic Conflict*
C. Fred Bergsten and Marcus Noland
June 1993 ISBN 0-88132-129-X

DISTRIBUTORS OUTSIDE THE UNITED STATES

Australia, New Zealand, and Papua New Guinea
D.A. Information Services
648 Whitehorse Road
Mitcham, Victoria 3132, Australia
tel: 61-3-9210-7777
fax: 61-3-9210-7788
e-mail: service@dadirect.com.au
http://www.dadirect.com.au

Canada
Renouf Bookstore
5369 Canotek Road, Unit 1
Ottawa, Ontario K1J 9J3, Canada
tel: 613-745-2665
fax: 613-745-7660
http://www.renoufbooks.com

United Kingdom and Europe
(including Russia and Turkey)
The Eurospan Group
3 Henrietta Street, Covent Garden
London WC2E 8LU England
tel: 44-20-7240-0856
fax: 44-20-7379-0609
http://www.eurospan.co.uk

India, Bangladesh, Nepal, and Sri Lanka
Viva Books Pvt.
Mr. Vinod Vasishtha
4325/3, Ansari Rd.
Daryaganj, New Delhi-110002
India
tel: 91-11-327-9280
fax: 91-11-326-7224
e-mail: vinod.viva@gndel.globalnet.
ems.vsnl.net.in

Japan and the Republic of Korea
United Publishers Services, Ltd.
Kenkyu-Sha Bldg.
9, Kanda Surugadai 2-Chome
Chiyoda-Ku, Tokyo 101
Japan
tel: 81-3-3291-4541
fax: 81-3-3292-8610
e-mail: saito@ups.co.jp
For trade accounts only.
Individuals will find IIE books in leading Tokyo bookstores.

Southeast Asia (Brunei, Cambodia, China, Malaysia, Hong Kong, Indonesia, Laos, Myanmar, the Philippines, Singapore, Taiwan, and Vietnam)
Hemisphere Publication Services
1 Kallang Pudding Rd. #04-03
Golden Wheel Building
Singapore 349316
tel: 65-741-5166
fax: 65-742-9356

Thailand
Asia Books
5 Sukhumvit Rd. Soi 61
Bangkok 10110 Thailand
tel: 662-714-0740-2 Ext: 221, 222, 223
fax: 662-391-2277
e-mail: purchase@asiabooks.co.th
http://www/asiabooksonline.com

Visit our Web site at:
http://www.iie.com
E-mail orders to:
orders@iie.com